WILLIAM GAMINARA

As a writer, William Gaminara's television work includes writing episodes for Jimmy McGovern's series *The Lakes*, BBC's *This Life* (winner of a Writers' Guild Drama Award), and a two-part adaptation of Rachel Morris's novel *Ella and the Mothers*. His stage plays include an adaptation of *Germinal* for Paines Plough, *Back up the Hearse* and *According to Hoyle* both for Hampstead Theatre, *The Three Lions* (Square Deal/PBJ Productions), which played at the Pleasance in London and at the Edinburgh Festival Fringe. He has translated two plays from French by Lionel Spycher for the Royal Court, *Pitbull* and *Nine and a Half Millimetres*.

As an actor, stage credits include Peter Stockmann in *Enemy of the People* (Chichester Festival Theatre), Pastor Paul in *The Christians* (Traverse Theatre/Gate Theatre), Major Groves in *Oppenheimer* (West End/RSC), Sir Roger Oatley *in The Shoemaker's Holiday* (RSC), Juror 10 in *12 Angry Men* (West End), Paul Watson in *The Body of an American* (Gate Theatre/Northampton), Sir John in *Less than Kind* (ATG tour), *Bloody Poetry* (Hampstead Theatre/Leicester Haymarket), *The Children's Hour* (National Theatre), amongst many others.

On television, his most recent work includes *Summer of Rockets*, *Catastrophe*, *Human Is*, *The Alienist* and *Father Brown*. He is probably best known as Professor Dalton in *Silent Witness* (eleven series), and on radio as Dr Richard Locke in *The Archers*.

William Gaminara

THE NIGHTINGALES

NICK HERN BOOKS

London

www.nickhernbooks.co.uk

A Nick Hern Book

The Nightingales first published in Great Britain in 2018 as a paperback original by Nick Hern Books Limited, The Glasshouse, 49a Goldhawk Road, London W12 8QP

The Nightingales copyright © 2018 William Gaminara

William Gaminara has asserted his right to be identified as the author of this work

Front cover: photography by Seamus Ryan; design by Bob King Creative

Designed and typeset by Nick Hern Books, London
Printed in Great Britain by Mimeo Ltd, Huntingdon, Cambridgeshire PE29 6XX

A CIP catalogue record for this book is available from the British Library

ISBN 978 1 84842 802 7

Woodland
CARBON
www.woodlandcarbon.co.uk
NICK HERN BOOKS
Printed on Carbon Captured paper

The Nightingales was produced by Jenny Topper and Theatre Royal Bath Productions, and first performed at Theatre Royal Bath on 7 November 2018, and subsequently performed at Cambridge Arts Theatre, New Theatre Cardiff, Chichester Festival Theatre and Malvern Theatres. The cast was as follows:

MAGGIE	Ruth Jones
STEVEN	Steven Pacey
DIANE	Mary Stockley
BEN	Philip McGinley
CONNIE	Sarah Earnshaw
BRUNO	Stefan Adegbola

Director	Christopher Luscombe
Designer	Jonathan Fensom
Lighting Designer	Nick Richings
Sound Designer	Jason Barnes
Musical Director	Luke Bateman
Movement Director	Jenny Arnold
Casting Director	Ginny Schiller CDG

Production Manager	Cath Bates
Company Stage Manager	Nick Earle
Deputy Stage Manager	Christopher Lambert
Assistant Stage Manager	Peggy Thomas

Characters

MAGGIE, *early fifties*
STEVEN, *sixty. RP. Married to Diane*
DIANE, *early forties. RP*
BEN, *mid- to late thirties. Yorkshire. Married to Connie*
CONNIE, *mid- to late thirties. Yorkshire*
BRUNO, *early thirties. RP. Black*

N.B. In the original production Maggie was Welsh but this is not essential. She could be anything but local to the village where the play is set.

This text went to press before the end of rehearsals and so may differ slightly from the play as performed.

ACT ONE

A middle-aged woman, MAGGIE, *steps forward and addresses the audience.*

MAGGIE. When we first arrived in the village we didn't really know anybody. I used to go to the shops on a Wednesday. Down past the church and along that little alley by the postbox. But then one day I tripped on the cobbles and went arse over, broke all the eggs. So I thought 'Right, I'm not doing this again'... and instead I started going the long way past the village hall. And that's when I heard them. Glorious it was. Lifted the spirits. After that I'd look forward to it. One week it would be Motown, then it would be... Mozart or... it was lovely, they really did make a lovely sound. I used to stop and listen outside. Sit down on the bench. Join in even. Secretly. (*Laughs*). Then one day I thought 'Sod this, I don't want to be on the outside any more. I want to be on the inside.' And I got up, walked to the door and just as I was about to go in I heard them all coming out. So then I nipped round the back and waited and sure enough out they came, all chatting and laughing. They seemed ever such a nice, friendly bunch. Which is why the following week I made sure that I arrived a bit earlier and I walked straight in bold as brass. (*Beat.*) Trouble is you never know with people do you, what they're really like. What they're capable of when they turn. Specially when they're spurred on by everyone around them. So yes, that was my mistake really...

The lights come up slowly on CONNIE, STEVEN *and* DIANE *in a small Yorkshire village hall. Stacked chairs in one corner and a piano. There is a main door, a side door leading to a kitchen (that we can see) and another door leading to a storeroom. The overhead light is not working. There is a ladder placed underneath it.* BEN *enters from the kitchen...*

BEN (*carrying a light bulb*). Well that's nice.

MAGGIE (*still to audience*). My big mistake…

CONNIE. What?

MAGGIE (*to audience*). Wanting to be on the inside.

BEN. Coffee's finished and the Jaffas have been nicked.

STEVEN. No!

The light fades on MAGGIE.

Who would steal the Jaffas?

BEN. Not to mention catshit on the kitchen mat.

CONNIE. Eugh! Who's in before us?

DIANE. It's usually the Scouts and then fruit-pickers on a Wednesday.

CONNIE. Fruit-pickers?

DIANE. Learning English.

BEN. The cat shat on the mat.

DIANE. Ha!

CONNIE. Probably one of the Scouts.

BEN. Shitting on the mat? I sincerely / hope not.

CONNIE. The Jaffas!

DIANE. Beats tying knots…

CONNIE. I can't sing till I have had a Jaffa. Coats the larynx. (*To* BEN.) Did you clear it up?

BEN. I'm on bulb duty if you hadn't noticed, Connie. Again.

STEVEN. Someone needs to take a proper look at those electrics. Before we all go up in smoke.

CONNIE. Bloody cat. I'm not touching it. (*To* DIANE.) Sorry. I just can't. It makes me… (*Retches*.)

STEVEN. You've had three kids!

CONNIE. Exactly.

BEN. They didn't shit on the floor!

CONNIE. I've done my fair share.

BEN. Not on a regular basis anyway.

DIANE. Don't worry, I'll / do it.

STEVEN. No, no, no... not... You do the music.

STEVEN goes into the kitchen.

CONNIE. You wouldn't catch Gareth Malone doing that.

Pause. We see STEVEN *clearing up the catshit and* BEN *climbing the ladder to change the light bulb.* DIANE *sorting out music.*

Remember that cruise?

BEN (*fitting the bulb*). Which one?

CONNIE (*to* DIANE). He was still playing tennis. It was some kind of freebie, three days in the Med... eat and drink as much you like. Thought I'd died and gone to heaven.

BEN *fits the bulb, comes down the ladder and tests the light.*

We stopped off in Barcelona. You know, in Spain...

BEN. Oh THAT Barcelona...

CONNIE. And there was us and all these Boy Scouts on some kind of a do. About two hundred of them I'm not exaggerating. Anyway, one of them recognised me from the Kellog's ad and before I knew it I was signing autographs for the next three hours. Remember that?

BEN. No.

CONNIE. You must do. I was pregnant with Georgie.

BEN. I don't.

The lights come on.

Wahay!

CONNIE. Why do you say that?

BEN. I don't remember!

CONNIE. You'd just gone out of some tournament, your knees were beginning to get really bad and to cheer us up, we went on a jolly.

BEN. I remember the cruise, I remember Barcelona... the one in Spain, I just don't remember the Boy Scouts.

CONNIE. Makes me sound like I'm making it up.

DIANE. Well the Scouts were definitely here today.

BEN. Better have a word with Akela.

STEVEN (*entering*). Sorted.

BEN. Give that man a medal.

CONNIE. Bruno is coming, isn't he?

DIANE. Yes. I mean... I assume so.

STEVEN. I jolly well hope so.

DIANE (*to* CONNIE). How's the house-hunting going?

CONNIE. Seeing a lovely place tomorrow.

BEN. Are we?

CONNIE. Wilton Avenue. Always wanted to live in an avenue.

STEVEN (*to* BEN). So you really are moving?

CONNIE. Yes.

BEN. Notice how I said that without moving my lips. Years of practice that.

STEVEN (*to* BEN). How's business?

BEN. Booming. Ish. Must be, we're moving house.

STEVEN. Anything of interest?

BEN. To you? Not really. I sold a bottle of Burgundy last week for nearly eight-fifty. Bought it three years ago for four hundred.

STEVEN. Really! In our household wine is strictly for drinking. (*Moving to the piano.*) Alright, everybody. I was waiting for Bruno but what the hell... the delightful and delectable 'Across the Alley'.

CONNIE. I've only just got it out of my head.

DIANE. It's catchy, isn't it.

CONNIE. Catchy? I've been humming it at four o'clock in the morning all week.

BEN. That's a relief. I thought the boiler was on the blink.

STEVEN gives them their notes on the piano.

STEVEN. Okay. Nice and bright. One, two , three / four...

He launches unexpectedly into 'Happy Birthday'. CONNIE and BEN (in the know) sing along. DIANE caught out.

DIANE. Oh no!

The song finishes.

You told them! You said you wouldn't!

CONNIE *and* BEN. Happy birthday!

BEN. Speech!

CONNIE produces a bottle of prosecco with a tag attached.

DIANE. It was meant to be a secret. Ah thank you.

BEN. Go on then.

DIANE. What?

BEN. How old?

CONNIE. You're as young as you feel.

BEN. So how young?

DIANE. Mind your own business.

BEN. You know he's got a big party planned, don't you.

DIANE. No he / hasn't

STEVEN. No I haven't.

BEN. One of those surprise dos when forty-three people jump out your wardrobe.

STEVEN. We don't even know forty-three people.

BEN. Go on how old?

CONNIE. Leave her alone.

DIANE. Old enough.

BEN. Twenty-six.

DIANE. I wish.

BEN. Fifty-two.

DIANE. Stop it.

BEN. What is it with women and age. It's just a number, isn't it. I'm not going to think any worse of you.

DIANE. I'm sure you're not it's just… it's just… I know it's silly but…

She takes a deep breath.

I'm forty-one. Okay? Forty-one.

CONNIE. That's nothing.

STEVEN. Tell me about it.

DIANE. I know, I know.

CONNIE. And you look fantastic. Doesn't she?

BEN. She does.

DIANE. Thank you.

BEN. For an old lady.

CONNIE. Stop it!

DIANE *laughs*. BRUNO *enters*.

BRUNO. I'm sorry, I'm sorry, I'm sorry…

BEN. Here he is…

BRUNO. Staff meeting ran over.

BEN. Up your Khyber.

CONNIE. Don't be vulgar.

STEVEN. It's ten past…

DIANE. He's not that late.

BRUNO. I'm beginning to realise I have a very stressful job.

BEN. Teaching? Piece of cake.

DIANE. You don't have Ofsted breathing down your neck.

BEN. Ofsted, schmoffsted.

BRUNO. So what have I missed?

BEN. Birthday girl.

BRUNO. I know! Happy birthday! (*Doesn't kiss her.*) What else?

CONNIE. Nothing.

DIANE. Clearing up the catshit.

BRUNO. If you hum it, I'll sing it.

    He and DIANE *laugh together.*

STEVEN (*playing a chord on the piano*). We're about to have a stab at 'Across the Alley'... when you're ready...

BEN. Bit high, isn't it?

STEVEN. It's in the same key as it was last time.

BEN. I reckon it was too high then.

STEVEN. It's definitely in your range.

BEN. Not in these trousers, it isn't...

MAGGIE (*off*). Hellooo!

STEVEN. If you change the key you change the whole... timbre of the thing.

BEN. Oh I wouldn't want to change the 'timbre'...

DIANE. Who's that?

MAGGIE (*off*). Argh! Ow!

BEN. It's Akela.

DIANE. Hello...?

BEN. Bringing back the Jaffas.

    DIANE *opens the door to reveal* MAGGIE *rubbing her foot.*

DIANE. Hello, can I help…

MAGGIE. Ow!

DIANE. Are you alright?

MAGGIE. You must think I'm completely… I've got an ingrown toenail and I just managed to stub it on that big step outside…

DIANE. Oh dear. Why don't you come in and sit down for a second?

MAGGIE. Do you mind if I do?

STEVEN. Of course not. Here…

He pulls up a chair.

MAGGIE. I'm so sorry, I'm interrupting you I know but I was standing outside listening… hoping that you'd be singing because you usually are only I couldn't actually hear anything so I just came in a bit closer. That's sounds awful, doesn't it, like I'm some sort of eavesdropper. Anyway I thought maybe I've got it wrong and there's no one in here but… oh yes then I heard 'Happy Birthday' and I saw you going in… so I knew someone was in here… And then I stubbed my flipping toe!

DIANE. Ouch.

MAGGIE. Yes ouch. But please, please just carry on. Pretend I'm not here.

STEVEN. Well we hadn't really got going yet.

MAGGIE (*to* CONNIE). We've met before…

CONNIE. Have we?

MAGGIE. You look very familiar.

CONNIE. I don't think so.

MAGGIE. I could have sworn…

DIANE. You've just moved in, haven't you…

MAGGIE. A month ago, yes.

DIANE. Thought so. Have you settled in alright?

MAGGIE. Oh yes. I'm sure we will. Takes a while, doesn't it. Listen tell me if I'm in your way, won't you.

STEVEN. It's absolutely fine but we only have the room for another hour so if you don't mind we'll crack on...

MAGGIE. Oh yes please do. You make such a lovely sound.

BRUNO. Flattery will get you everywhere.

MAGGIE. Whose birthday is it if you don't mind my...

DIANE. Oh mine.

MAGGIE. Aah. Happy birthday.

DIANE. Thank you.

STEVEN. Right. From the top... on our feet... by special request. For?

MAGGIE. Oh. Maggie...

STEVEN. For Maggie.

DIANE. For Maggie's toe.

> STEVEN *gives them their starting notes. They launch into 'Across the Alley from the Alamo' (The Mills Brothers) singing a capella. They sing well.* MAGGIE *listens enraptured. At the end she bursts into applause.*

MAGGIE (*to* STEVEN). What a voice!

BEN. Thank you.

> *They all laugh.*

MAGGIE. All of you.

STEVEN. Bit slow.

MAGGIE. That was fantastic!

STEVEN. My fault. But we're getting there...

MAGGIE. I think you've got there!

BEN. Still too high.

MAGGIE. How long have you been together?

BEN. Too long.

BRUNO. Do you sing?

MAGGIE. Me!?

CONNIE. Course she does!

MAGGIE. No.

BEN. Great, you're in.

CONNIE. Just listen to her speak.

MAGGIE. I mean I CAN sing but... no I'm a pianist really, at least I was when I was a child... quite gifted actually but... my mother wasn't very keen, then I damaged my hand and what with one thing and another... Long story.

CONNIE. We chat more than we sing.

BEN. YOU do.

DIANE. How's the toe?

MAGGIE. The toe? Oh the...! There you are, see!

DIANE. The power of music.

MAGGIE. You just go somewhere else, don't you.

DIANE. You certainly do.

STEVEN. Strauss and Mozart actively lower your blood pressure. Anyway...

MAGGIE (*to* CONNIE). We have definitely met before. (*To* STEVEN.) Sorry. (*To* CONNIE.) I never forget a face.

DIANE. Telly.

MAGGIE. Oh! I see. Now I feel all stupid. Are you an actress then?

CONNIE. Well...

BEN. No.

CONNIE. No... not... not as such but I have done some modelling.

STEVEN. She's being modest, she was a Bond girl once.

MAGGIE. You weren't!

BEN. She wasn't.

STEVEN. Sort of.

BEN. UniBond maybe.

CONNIE. I was in one scene of one film.

MAGGIE. Oh I love Daniel Craig.

CONNIE. Before him actually.

MAGGIE. Not Timothy Dalton!

BEN. Steady. She's not THAT old.

MAGGIE. Oh I'm sorry I didn't / mean...

CONNIE. Pierce Brosnan.

MAGGIE. Did you get to meet him?

CONNIE. Oh yes! We were in the same scene.

MAGGIE. No!

CONNIE. Yes, it was a scene around a pool and I had to get up,
off this lounger and walk across the back of the shot.
Nothing... you know. But we had to do it eight times. Pierce
said I kept making him forget his lines. Always remember that.

MAGGIE. You would, wouldn't you. Maybe it's from that then.

Pause.

Although...

CONNIE. Ambre Solaire? I did a big campaign / for them.

MAGGIE. You weren't in Lidl's last Wednesday, were you...

CONNIE. Er...

MAGGIE. And you dropped a bottle of ketchup at the checkout
desk...

CONNIE. Oh right. Yes, no I...

MAGGIE. What a mess!

CONNIE. Yes, you're right that / was me.

BEN *laughing*.

MAGGIE. I knew it! I never forget a face. I remember bumping into a schoolfriend of mine. Hadn't seen her for thirty years, hadn't even given her a second's thought and I recognised her instantly. And you know what, she knew exactly who I was. She even remembered the date of my birthday.

CONNIE. Right...

MAGGIE. 7th of Feb.

CONNIE (*to* BEN). What's so funny?

BEN. Nothing, nothing.

MAGGIE. I thought for a moment they were going to charge you for it.

CONNIE. What?

MAGGIE. The ketchup.

CONNIE. Oh... no. They didn't.

MAGGIE. Good.

STEVEN. If you don't mind we'll keep going but you're very welcome to stay.

MAGGIE. Thank you but I've got a doctor's appointment.

STEVEN. Dr Brewer?

MAGGIE. Er...

STEVEN. Evening surgery?

MAGGIE. Yes.

BRUNO. Dr Brewer. One eyebrow. Straight across both eyes. Bit scary.

MAGGIE. Is he?

BRUNO. She.

MAGGIE. No!

BRUNO. 'Fraid so.

MAGGIE. Anyway, nice to have met you all. See you!

Goodbyes from everyone. She exits.

STEVEN. Okay...

MAGGIE *reappears almost immediately.*

MAGGIE. Can I ask you a huge favour? Would you mind if I came and listened again?

STEVEN. Any objections?

STEVEN *turns to the others. Everyone is fine about it.*

There you go. Nem. con. A glutton for punishment.

Blackout. Lights up on BRUNO *seated in a chair. He addresses an unseen interviewer.*

BRUNO. Favourite colour? Black. No two ways about it. I'm not just saying it because I AM black. The right kind of black. I know, I know... that sounds weird but there are different shades of black. Jet. Coal. Onyx. Olive. Ebony. See? Depends what mood I'm in. But just put black. Favourite singer. Easy. Luther Vandross. (*Beat.*) You've never heard of Luther Vandross?! You're kidding me! 'Never Too Much'? (*Sings a few lines from 'Never Too Much' by Luther Vandross.*) No? You need to have words with your dad, mate. (*Beat.*) Ambition. Simple. To outlive my mother. Next? (*Beat.*) What does the...? (*Beat.*) What does the group mean to me? Oh man, where do I begin. Seriously. When I moved to Tapley, to be honest it wasn't out of choice. But I used to come on holiday near here with my mum... she has connections here... so I knew what to expect. And the fact is I do like the countryside. I like the fields and the fresh air. I like... tractors, everything. The only problem was the people. A week after I got here I went for a run round some of the lanes. When I got back, there was a police helicopter overhead. I kid you not. A helicopter! Because so many people had reported seeing a suspicious-looking character. But you know the second I joined this group, I felt I belonged. They've been great. It's like one big family. Squabbling the whole time. But in a healthy kind of way – (*Laughs.*) Seriously I would take a bullet for any one of them.

Lights up on the main room in the hall. BEN *is seated at a piano playing chopsticks badly.* CONNIE (*eating a Jaffa Cake*) *and* DIANE *sat nearby.*

DIANE. Nine years.

CONNIE. What?

BRUNO (*still to interviewer*). A rubber bullet obviously.

DIANE. Since we started.

CONNIE. Is it really?

DIANE. To the day. According to Steven. I hadn't been very well. Wasn't really up for socialising. So we went out for lunch and on the way back Steven said he had to drop in at the village hall for something or other. When we came in there were a couple of friends already here mucking around on the piano. And next thing I knew we were all singing songs. He'd organised it all of course. To cheer me up.

CONNIE. Ah. I don't think we were even in the village yet, were we, Ben? (*To* BEN, *re: his playing.*) Can you stop doing that?

DIANE. Feels like another lifetime.

CONNIE. What was I doing nine years ago? Oh yes, exactly the same as I'm doing now. Silly me.

BEN. This piano needs tuning. Either that or I need tuning.

CONNIE. It's you.

BEN. You reckon? Maybe I should get one of them blind fellas to stick a spanner up me jacksie... have a quick tweak.

MAGGIE *enters.*

Hello, gorgeous.

CONNIE. Hi.

DIANE. Hello.

MAGGIE. I've missed it, haven't I. Or have I?

CONNIE. As good as.

DIANE. Bruno didn't turn up.

MAGGIE. Oh bum. I thought it was Tuesday today. Up until an hour ago I actually thought it was Tuesday. How stupid can you get.

BEN. Ask her.

MAGGIE. And then I fell asleep.

DIANE. I hope he's alright.

BEN. You know what, you're like our very own fifth Beatle.

MAGGIE. FIFTH Beatle. Am I?

BEN. Yes.

MAGGIE. Blimey. Which one was that?

BEN. The one after the fourth.

MAGGIE. I thought there WERE only four.

BEN. I know but...

CONNIE. Ignore him, Maggie.

DIANE. There are only two, aren't there.

CONNIE. Two Beatles!

BEN. Jesus.

DIANE. Left I mean.

BEN. I'm out of my depth.

DIANE. I always thought they were rather overrated.

BEN. The Beatles!

    STEVEN *enters on the phone*.

STEVEN. Bruno didn't say anything at all to you, did he, Diane?

DIANE. When?

STEVEN. The other night. In the pub. (*Beat.*) I thought you ran / into him...

DIANE. Oh. No. No he didn't.

BEN. Your wife thinks The Beatles are overrated!

DIANE. Is that not allowed?

STEVEN (*on the phone*). Bruno. Me again. Just making sure you're okay… give us a call. (*Ends call.*) Right that's that. Hello, Maggie.

MAGGIE. I thought it was Tuesday.

BEN. So are we done and dusted or what?

STEVEN. Up to you really. There's not a lot more we can do.

MAGGIE. I could kick myself.

She produces Tupperware from her bag and puts it on the piano.

I even made flapjacks.

CONNIE. Ooh.

MAGGIE. Seems a shame to waste them. Jack's favourite. And his dad's, for that matter.

CONNIE. Oh go on then.

She takes one.

What's your husband's name?

MAGGIE. Oh he's long gone, I'm afraid.

CONNIE. Right.

MAGGIE. Haven't had much luck with men.

CONNIE. Me neither.

MAGGIE. They come and then they go.

CONNIE. Yeah? I've got the opposite problem.

STEVEN (*re: flapjacks*). We'll take some. (*To* CONNIE.) The grandchildren are coming over for the weekend. They'll make short work of them.

MAGGIE. You look too young to have grandchildren, Diane.

DIANE. They're not mine.

STEVEN. Wife number one.

MAGGIE. Oh I see.

STEVEN. Four children and six grandchildren. About to be seven.

MAGGIE. Seven!

BEN. He's the Rod Stewart of Tapley, aren't you...

STEVEN. If you say so.

MAGGIE *laughing*.

MAGGIE. He's funny, your fella.

CONNIE. Oh he's hilarious.

MAGGIE. My second husband was a comedian.

CONNIE. Oh?

MAGGIE. He used to have me in stitches. For a while anyway. He could just sit and tell jokes one after the other. Didn't matter if there were ten people in the room or two. Shortest marriage in the history of marriages I reckon. He ran off with the girl doing the catering at the reception.

CONNIE. Really?

MAGGIE. Honest to God.

BEN. The wedding reception?

MAGGIE. Yes. Not on the day itself but four days later.

BEN. Four days!

MAGGIE. I don't think he ever really wanted to get married. Not to me anyway. I even wrote to the *Guinness Book of Records* but they never got back. I think I must have got the wrong address. I can't imagine anyone beating that, can you?

BEN. Short of copping off with the vicar, not really.

MAGGIE. Anyway, I've got my lovely boy and that's what matters. So what about you, Diane, do you not / have any...

DIANE. No. Not of my own. Not... (*Beat.*) no.

MAGGIE. Right. Not too late though is it, nowadays.

DIANE. Well...

STEVEN. I think four's enough.

MAGGIE. A woman of sixty-two gave birth the other day.

DIANE. Really?

MAGGIE. In Basildon!

CONNIE. Hard work.

MAGGIE. It is when you're on your own.

Pause. BEN *is getting something out of his bag.*

STEVEN. Right. Are we off?

DIANE. Shouldn't we wait?

STEVEN. There's only fifteen minutes left.

BEN *hands* STEVEN *a photo.*

What's this?

BEN. A QE11 error.

STEVEN. Right.

BEN. It's an RSPCA silver with a little kitten on the front.

STEVEN. And?

BEN. They only went and left the Queen's head off it.

STEVEN. Very careless. Have you got one of those?

BEN. I'm getting a couple of singles. Mint condition.

STEVEN. Mounted?

BEN. Unmounted. Eight hundred each. If you're interested?

STEVEN. I might well be.

BEN. They've doubled in value in the last five years.

BRUNO *enters. Cheers and jeers.*

STEVEN. What the hell happened to you?

DIANE. Thank God for that.

BRUNO. I know, I know. Apologies, everyone. But first the carer was late, then Mum had a fall, and then... believe me you don't want to know...

DIANE. Is she alright?

BRUNO. Shaken but she'll live. Totally out of my control. Sorry.

STEVEN. And your phone was off.

DIANE. At least he's okay.

STEVEN. Hardly worth coming…

BRUNO. *Except…* on the plus side… I am the bearer of glad tidings.

STEVEN. What?

CONNIE. You've won the lottery.

BRUNO. I wish.

BEN. You've got a girlfriend.

BRUNO. Er… not that I'm aware of, no.

CONNIE. Give us a clue.

BRUNO. I have one word to say. Talentfest.

BEN. Talentfest.

BRUNO. Yes.

MAGGIE. Oh I read about that.

DIANE. Never heard of it.

STEVEN. Nor have I.

BRUNO. Oh come on! Talentfest! Okay. So *Britain's Got Talent*. You've heard of that?

DIANE. Of course.

BRUNO. It's like that… only it's live. So all over the country they hold heats, singing, dancing, whatever you want to do

CONNIE. Oh yes!

BRUNO. …and if you win your heat you go on to the grand final.

CONNIE. In Blackpool.

BRUNO. In Blackpool.

CONNIE. How do you apply?

BRUNO. Easy. You send in a recording. Or more to the point WE send / in a …

STEVEN. No way.

BRUNO. Why not!

MAGGIE. Oh go on!

BEN. No chance.

DIANE. Where is it happening?

BRUNO. Leeds. It's a no-brainer.

BEN. It is if you've got no brain.

STEVEN. We're grown-ups, for God's sake. I'm sixty years old, why would I be interested in entering a third-rate talent show?

CONNIE. Third-rate? I don't think so.

MAGGIE. Not even second-rate.

STEVEN. Hanging on every word of some so-called 'celebrity' masquerading as a musical genius… I mean why?

DIANE. For a laugh.

BRUNO. And because we'd win it.

STEVEN. I'm afraid we wouldn't win it.

BEN. We're not good enough.

CONNIE. Says who?

MAGGIE. I think you are. I think you'd win hands down.

BRUNO. It would make a change from the Christmas concert.

DIANE. And it would be fun!

STEVEN. Singing is fun. We get that here, don't we? Is that not enough?

CONNIE. Is there an audience?

BRUNO. Yes. It's proper. If you win you get through to the final and if you win THAT… virtually automatic qualification for *Britain's Got Talent*.

CONNIE. No!

DIANE. We would have to rehearse more.

BEN. Forget it.

CONNIE. Why not?

BEN. I'm busy.

CONNIE. Doing what?

BEN. Working, in case you hadn't noticed.

CONNIE. I hadn't actually. Some of us do proper jobs.

STEVEN. I'm with Ben.

CONNIE. Oh don't be such spoilsports.

BEN. You're the one who wants to move house.

MAGGIE. There was a young boy the last place I lived who got through to the final. First he got an agent, then he got a record deal and THEN he ended up on telly. And he didn't even win, he came second.

CONNIE. Really!

MAGGIE. He's rolling in it now.

BEN. Yeah?

MAGGIE. Literally rolling. And look at that Susan Boyle, she came from nowhere, didn't she. I'm not saying you're nowhere…

BEN. We are.

MAGGIE. I'm just… you know. You could be the next Susan Boyle.

STEVEN. Maggie, why would I want to be the next Susan Boyle?

CONNIE. You'd wouldn't mind her bank balance, would you.

BEN. True.

MAGGIE. She's a multimillionaire now. Multi.

BRUNO. I rest my case.

CONNIE (*exiting at speed*). Just thinking about it makes me want to wee.

DIANE (*to* STEVEN). It would look good on your applications.

STEVEN. Really?

DIANE. Of course it would. If we got somewhere. When is it?

BRUNO. 28th August.

MAGGIE. I think you should go for it. Why wouldn't you? It's not as if you get a chance like that every day is it. When I was little my dad used to say to me 'If opportunity doesn't knock, then build a door.' I never really understood what it meant at the time but I do now and it sounds to me like you should be building doors. I'd give my right arm to be on *Britain's Got Talent*. If I had a talent. Even if I DIDN'T have a talent. I mean, what have you got to lose?

Pause. All thinking.

BRUNO. Let's have a vote.

BEN. Here we go.

STEVEN. Well this has to be unanimous.

BRUNO. All those in favour… (*Opening the door.*) Connie!

DIANE. Connie's definitely up for it.

BEN. Connie's in the final already. She's halfway to Vegas.

BRUNO. All in favour…

CONNIE *enters.*

CONNIE. Wait for me, wait for me! What are we voting for…?

BEN. Whether or not to bomb North Korea.

BRUNO. Talentfest. One, two, three…

Everyone, bar STEVEN, BEN and MAGGIE, puts their hands up.

CONNIE (*to* BEN). Put your hand up.

BEN. What?

CONNIE. You heard.

BEN. Free vote this.

CONNIE. Put your bloody hand up!

BEN *puts his hand up. They all look at a reluctant* STEVEN.

BEN. I should stick your hand up, Maggie, unless you want your head cut off.

MAGGIE *starts to raise her hand.*

STEVEN. With all due respect, Maggie is not in the group.

MAGGIE. No Steven's right... I mean I WOULD... but no... he's absolutely right...

DIANE. Come on, Steven, don't spoil it for everyone.

STEVEN, *reluctant, but not wanting to spoil it for everyone.*

BEN. No pressure.

DIANE. It'll be fun.

STEVEN. Will it?

ALL. Yes!

BEN. No.

STEVEN. Alright, alright. Against my better judgement...

He puts his hand up. They all cheer.

But if we do it, we do it properly. Nothing half-baked.

DIANE. Of course not.

CONNIE. You won't regret it. Trust me.

BEN. Right can we go home now.

They begin to disperse.

CONNIE. I've got a real feeling about this. I think we could be going somewhere.

BEN. Based on what exactly?

CONNIE. It's a gut feeling.

BEN. Ah. One of those.

CONNIE. You don't have them.

BEN. Don't I? You should go and see Dr Brewer with all your gut feelings. Come on.

MAGGIE. Oh she was amazing.

BEN. Who?

MAGGIE. Dr Brewer.

BRUNO. I warned you, didn't I. Scary or what.

MAGGIE. She is a bit. You'd think she'd... shave it or pluck it or something.

BRUNO. Yes, just the bit in the middle. For a firebreak if nothing else.

MAGGIE. Trouble is you stop listening, don't you. There she was going on about this... lump or whatever she'd found and I was just sat there staring at this... doormat on her face.

BRUNO. Yeah.

Silence.

DIANE. A lump?

MAGGIE. Yes.

Silence. She is aware of them all looking at her.

Oh nothing... you know. Just...

She indicates her left breast.

DIANE. Oh Maggie.

BEN. I'm sorry to hear that.

MAGGIE. Oh it's nothing serious. A cyst or lipoma or whatever.

DIANE. Even so.

MAGGIE. But what a palaver. I've been up the hospital half the week. Scans and all sorts.

DIANE. Why didn't you say?

MAGGIE. Weeell…

DIANE. Us all wittering on about nothing.

CONNIE. Is it large?

MAGGIE. No! No, don't get me wrong, it's the size of a pea. I wouldn't have bothered only she insisted.

DIANE. Better to be safe.

STEVEN. I'm sure it'll be fine.

DIANE. They usually are.

MAGGIE. I'm not worried. Just sore. They had to take a little bit to test. I nearly passed out when I saw the size of the needle.

CONNIE. Do you need help with Jack?

MAGGIE. No I'm fine. Really. It's just waiting for the results. To see if it's 'friendly' or not. Makes you a bit jumpy. A friendly lump. (*Laughing.*) I thought they were talking about me at first. Right, I must be off…

She heads for the door.

…don't forget the flapjacks. I made them myself.

DIANE. Let us know if there's anything we can do.

MAGGIE. It'll be fine. They were ever so nice up there…

STEVEN. Thank God for the NHS.

MAGGIE. I'll say. Bye, all.

MAGGIE exits. DIANE is preoccupied.

STEVEN (*privately*). You okay?

She nods.

Sure?

DIANE. Yes.

CONNIE. Rather her than me. I'm not good with needles either.

STEVEN. As she says, probably nothing.

BRUNO. Anyone coming for a drink?

DIANE. Why not? Steven?

STEVEN. I can't. I've got things to do. / For tomorrow.

DIANE. Oh of course.

STEVEN. I did tell you.

DIANE. Sorry I forgot. I'll lock up.

STEVEN (*handing her a key*). Okay.

CONNIE. What's happening tomorrow?

BRUNO (*to* DIANE). See you in there? Bye, all.

    BRUNO *exits*. STEVEN *getting ready to leave*.

DIANE. He's been shortlisted for the choir at St Michael's.

CONNIE. Really?

BEN. Traitor.

STEVEN. I'd still do all this. See you later.

CONNIE. Good luck!

STEVEN. Bye.

    He exits. CONNIE *still getting her stuff together.*

BEN. Come on! I'm going to miss the footie.

CONNIE. Oh God forbid! Cos you've only ever seen twenty-eight thousand games on telly before. And they're all so different, aren't they.

BEN. They are actually. To the trained eye.

CONNIE. Really? I must have missed that one.

BEN. What one?

CONNIE. The one where there weren't twenty-four men in stripy shirts kicking a ball around.

BEN. Twenty-four?!

CONNIE *starts clearing up the coffee cups.*

DIANE. Don't worry, I'll do those.

CONNIE. Sure?

DIANE. Yes.

BEN. Unless the ref's having a really bad day I think you'll find there are generally twenty-two.

CONNIE. Same difference.

BEN. And they're not always stripy, as it happens.

CONNIE. Really? Amazing what the trained / eye can see…

BEN. Come on… see ya.

DIANE. Bye.

CONNIE. Bye.

They exit. DIANE *takes the cups into the kitchen. She checks herself in the mirror. After a moment* BRUNO *walks through the swing doors.*

BRUNO. Rotarians?

DIANE. Cancelled.

BRUNO. Fruit-pickers?

DIANE. Been and gone.

They move towards each other and kiss passionately. Blackout.

Lights up on CONNIE, BEN *and* STEVEN *in the hall.*

STEVEN. You know I'm wondering whether we shouldn't try some of the classical stuff again. Just to shake things up a bit.

CONNIE. Such as?

STEVEN. Byrd, Gesualdo…

CONNIE. Who?

STEVEN. The man who put the mad in 'Madrigal'.

BEN. He murdered his wife.

DIANE (*entering*). Who did?

BEN. Gesualdo.

CONNIE. Did he?

BEN. According to Steven.

STEVEN. It's true.

CONNIE. Yeah well don't get any ideas.

BEN. Too late.

CONNIE. Ben wants to do the Sounds of the Sixties...

BEN. And? You wanted to do the B-sides of A-sides.

DIANE. What's wrong with that?

BEN. B-sides are always terrible.

CONNIE. No they're not.

BEN. Yes they are. That's why they're B-sides.

Suddenly, a hand appears round the door waving a piece of paper... we hear BRUNO *before we see him...*

BRUNO (*off*). I have here in my hand... a letter from Herr Louis Walsh...

CONNIE. Louis Walsh!

STEVEN. Remind me who Louis Walsh is?

BRUNO. I cannot believe you're asking that.

BEN. Poor man's Simon Cowell.

DIANE. He wouldn't write it himself surely.

BRUNO *enters.*

BRUNO (*reads*). 'Thank you for sending in your audition reel... we've been inundated with applications beyond our expectations. Nevertheless the panel would very much like to invite you to participate in the forthcoming Talentfest heat.'

DIANE. Yes.

CONNIE. We did it!

BEN. They must be desperate.

CONNIE. They're lucky to have us.

DIANE. Well done, Bruno.

BRUNO. I didn't do anything.

DIANE. Yes you did.

BRUNO. This changes everything, you realise.

STEVEN. It certainly does.

BRUNO. For one thing we are going to need moves.

BEN. And babysitters.

BRUNO. Just stop having babies.

STEVEN. Moves?

> BRUNO *has a quick dance.*

CONNIE. Yes!

BEN. Bloody hell!

BRUNO. Well we can't just stand there and sing.

STEVEN. Why not? That's what most singers do.

DIANE. They don't. They perform, they… you know.

STEVEN. We're not dancers. At least I'M not.

BEN. Abba didn't move. They did alright.

BRUNO. Abba didn't move?!

BEN. They might have… swayed.

BRUNO. They did more than sway. Anyway they weren't a capella.

DIANE. Early-morning rehearsals…

BEN. I can't speak before nine let alone sing.

CONNIE. What about clothes? What are we going to wear?

STEVEN. What are we going to SING?

CONNIE. Is it televised?

BRUNO. No.

CONNIE. What about the final?

BEN. Connie, we haven't reached the final, we haven't / even...

CONNIE. I know.

BRUNO. Of course THAT'S televised.

DIANE. But there's a live audience for this?

BRUNO. For the heat, yes. They sell tickets!

CONNIE. Oh my God. (*Crossing legs.*) It's gone straight to my bladder...

DIANE. I'll make a list...

STEVEN. Of what?

DIANE. What we need to be thinking about...

STEVEN. Why can't we just get up and sing...

DIANE (*writing down*). Clothes, choreography...

BEN. 'Choreography'! It was 'moves' a minute ago.

BRUNO. There's an old sound system somewhere in the building I think.

DIANE. Microphones?

STEVEN. Oh Lord.

BRUNO. I'll see what I can borrow from school.

MAGGIE *enters*.

MAGGIE. Guess what.

CONNIE. We / know!

MAGGIE. I couldn't stop beaming when I heard. It's just the best news you could possibly hope for...

CONNIE. Absolutely...

MAGGIE (*beat*). You know? How could you... How did you know?

DIANE. Bruno's just told us.

MAGGIE. But… (*Realising*.) I've just had the all-clear.
Completely clear.

Pause.

CONNIE (*realising*). Oh! Oh right… fantastic.

DIANE (*giving* MAGGIE *a hug*). That is wonderful news!

MAGGIE. It is.

DIANE. What a relief!

MAGGIE. Yes. I knew it would be alright really. But you can't
help worrying, can you.

DIANE. Of course not.

DIANE *overwhelmed*.

MAGGIE. Are you okay?

DIANE. Yes! Sorry, I'm… I'm just delighted for you.

BEN. Wonderful.

CONNIE. You can forget all about it now.

BRUNO. Great news all round. Take a look at that.

He hands MAGGIE *the letter. She reads.*

Louis Walsh no less.

MAGGIE. No!

BRUNO. Yes.

MAGGIE. They want you!

BRUNO. They're begging us.

MAGGIE. How exciting! You're going to need a name now,
aren't you.

BEN. 'Northlife.'

CONNIE. Don't be silly.

BEN. 'Take This.'

STEVEN. Not right now we don't, shall we get started?

MAGGIE *produces a Tupperware box.*

MAGGIE. And to cap it all… (*To* BEN.) Ginger nuts.

BEN. Yes but don't tell anyone.

They both laugh.

MAGGIE. I can't tell you how relieved I'm feeling.

DIANE. I bet.

STEVEN. Right. First things first. It seems August 28th is now
a date so I suggest whatever we choose to sing should be
something reasonably familiar.

BEN. Such as?

STEVEN. Either 'Only You', 'Trust Not' or… and I think this
would tick every box… 'You Raise Me Up'.

CONNIE. Too hard.

BEN. Yeah.

STEVEN. No it's not. Anyway they're all old friends, as it
were. Have a think over the next few days, then let me know
your first and second choice. In the meantime…

He plays a chord on the piano.

DIANE. Maggie, why don't you sing?

MAGGIE. Me! No…

ALL. Yes! / Come on…

MAGGIE. I'm not… no!

BRUNO. Go on. We're only warming up, aren't we. Join in.

STEVEN. Yes. The more the merrier.

MAGGIE. I'll put you off.

BEN. Who cares.

CONNIE. We're unputoffable. It's one of our USPs.

BEN. You can't have more than one USP.

CONNIE. I can. I can have as many as I like.

BEN. They'd just be SPs wouldn't they.

CONNIE. What!?

DIANE. You're celebrating.

BRUNO. We all are.

MAGGIE. I'm not sure I know any of your songs...

BRUNO. Of course you do. Beatles?

BEN. Not really up to it. Are they, Diane?

DIANE. Ha Ha. Everly Brothers.

BRUNO. 'Dream, Dream, Dream'... everybody knows that.

MAGGIE. But I don't know any of the... what's-its, you know.

STEVEN. Harmonies? Don't worry. Make them up. They do.

STEVEN starts playing.

BRUNO. Just sing the main tune...

MAGGIE. Really?

They start all singing together in harmony and, gradually, as
MAGGIE *gets more confident, they let her continue with the*
lead solo line and start doing a capella around her. Eventually
STEVEN *stops playing the piano.* MAGGIE *in seventh*
heaven... she has a decent voice and by the end is flying.
At the end they all break out into applause... She is radiant.

Was that alright?

ALL. Yes! / Fantastic...

MAGGIE. I'm out of breath. Was I out of tune?

BEN. Never stopped me.

MAGGIE. So I was.

DIANE. No!

BRUNO. You've got a lovely voice.

STEVEN. Pitch-perfect.

MAGGIE. You know what… this is going to sound mad but I'll say it anyway… when we started, it felt like all these invisible hands were holding me up… supporting me… and then once we got going… I could feel the hands slowly moving away, ever so gently… and it felt like I was flying. Actually flying!

Blackout.

Lights up in the kitchen. BRUNO *lies on top of* DIANE. *They have just finished having sex and are breathing heavily.*

BRUNO. That was good. That was so good. You?

DIANE. Yes.

BRUNO. No splinters?

DIANE. God I hope not. A hard one to explain. No one over forty should have to have sex on a table.

BRUNO. Good thing I'm so strong.

DIANE. You are!

He starts to withdraw.

No, no… stay! Just for a bit longer.

Pause.

I bet you're brilliant at sport.

BRUNO. I am actually yes.

DIANE. Which ones?

BRUNO. Tennis. Squash.

DIANE. Good hand-eye coordination.

BRUNO. You noticed.

They laugh.

All brawn and no brain.

DIANE. That's not true. I know that for a fact. You don't get a first from Bristol unless you're smart.

BRUNO. How did you know that?

DIANE. You must have told me.

BRUNO. Did I? Christ. Short-term memory. I hope it's not genetic.

DIANE. Don't. How is she?

BRUNO. Struggling.

DIANE. I'm sorry. I didn't...

She freezes. She thinks she has heard a noise... then relaxes.

I keep expecting a pack of Scouts to come crashing in.

BRUNO. One way of finding out about the birds and the bees.

Pause.

Do you mind my asking you something?

DIANE. What?

BRUNO. Have you done this before?

DIANE. No. No I haven't.

BRUNO. Ever? While you've been with Steven, I mean.

DIANE. Never.

BRUNO. So why now?

DIANE *(beat)*. I just wanted to. Needed to.

Pause.

BRUNO. What would he do? If he found out. Only we are going to be rehearsing more and more...

DIANE. I know.

They kiss.

We have a sort of...

BRUNO *(beat)*. What?

DIANE. I don't know...

BRUNO. Understanding?

DIANE. No. Not exactly…

BRUNO. He doesn't know about this? He doesn't know about me!

DIANE. No!

BRUNO. You're quite sure?

DIANE. Yes.

BRUNO. That would be… I'd find that difficult. Not that I find this easy. So it's what… an understanding that he doesn't know about or…?

DIANE. No! It's not an understanding as such. He's a lot older than me and… we don't have a very active sex life.

BRUNO. Right.

DIANE. I mean we do have sex but just / not…

BRUNO. And that's what this is, is it? Sex.

DIANE. No! God no.

BRUNO. Only…

Pause.

DIANE. What?

BRUNO. When this first happened it felt like sex. Good sex but still just sex. And now… it feels like it's more than that. A lot more.

Silence.

Oh God.

DIANE. What?

BRUNO. You've gone very quiet.

DIANE. No I was / just…

BRUNO. I suppose I just wanted to know whether you felt the same way. Or even a similar way. Or maybe this is still just sex for you.

DIANE (*beat*). It never was.

BRUNO. I can't tell you how good it is to hear you say that.

BRUNO *kisses her.*

DIANE. How long do we have?

BRUNO. Ten minutes.

DIANE. You'll have to be quick then.

She pulls him towards her. The lights fade.

Blackout. Snap lighting change to STEVEN *sitting in a chair.*

STEVEN (*spelling*). D–E–L–L–E–R... Alfred Deller. Direct descendant... musically speaking... of Farinelli. Farinelli? No? Product of the single most criminal practice in the history of classical music. Over a period of about a hundred years tens of thousands of boys were emasculated. In Italy this is. Genitally mutilated. Poor boys, from families in the south. Out of a family of ten or twelve children, one at the age of six or seven would be sacrificed to the knife. In the hope that he might lift them out of poverty by becoming... effectively the next Michael Jackson... you have heard of Michael Jackson I trust. Yes good. But there was no guarantee. For every three thousand that were castrated, only about a hundred made the grade. The rest became social rejects. So there you are. Short question, long answer. Deller it is. (*Beat.*) Colour. Blue I think.

DIANE *arrives and sits next to him.*

DIANE. Sorry.

STEVEN. Where have you been?

DIANE. Got held up.

STEVEN. Right. Only... right. Yes, so blue. What else? Ambition... no, nothing really.

DIANE. Yes you do.

STEVEN. What?

DIANE. You'd like to run a choir.

STEVEN. Well yes, I suppose so. If it happens it happens. As for the group... I've said it before, I'll say it again music is my lifeblood. Always has been. I could no more exist without it than I could without food or water. Or for that matter without Diane. (*Beat.*) Your turn.

DIANE. Number... eight. Colour... yellow. Singer... tricky... no, no not Tricky... I mean, it's difficult... Probably Ella Fitzgerald... (*Beat. Clarifies.*) FITZGERALD. Ambition?

Pause.

To have a baby.

STEVEN *reacts.*

What?

Pause.

What? Should I not say that, is that too... honest? (*Beat.*) Okay forget it, miss that one out. What does the group mean to me?... Er... It keeps me sane I suppose. That's the theory anyway. Takes my mind off other things. For a couple of hours. Things like... things like...

Pause.

Things like wanting to have a baby.

Blackout. Out of the darkness, we hear live a capella singing of 'You Raise Me Up'. The lights half-fade up on BRUNO, DIANE, STEVEN, CONNIE and BEN all singing round the piano. STEVEN is conducting, BRUNO is singing the lead. There is a ladder beneath the main light. MAGGIE, unseen, is in a storeroom to one side.

BRUNO sings the first two lines of the chorus of 'You Raise Me Up'.

STEVEN. No, Ben! You're meant to be coming in straight after 'seas'.

BEN. Oh sod it.

STEVEN (*singing*). '...to walk on stormy seas ON STORMY SEAS...' Count it. If you can't feel it, count it. And concentrate.

MAGGIE (*offstage*). Bayonet or screw?

BEN. What?

MAGGIE *enters carrying two bulbs*.

MAGGIE. Bayonet or screw?

BEN. Oh. I thought I'd got lucky for a minute...

STEVEN. Please focus, everyone!

BEN. Bayonet.

STEVEN. Once more from bar ten. One, two, three and...

MAGGIE *climbs the ladder and changes the bulb during the following*.

BRUNO (*singing*). 'You raise me up so I can...'

STEVEN. You're sharp...

BRUNO. Sharp? Never have been before.

STEVEN. Yes well we have to be a little bit more exacting now.

BRUNO. A LITTLE bit...

STEVEN. Right, let's try / again...

BEN. I need a leak.

STEVEN. Oh for God's sake!

BEN. I need a leak. What can I say!

CONNIE. You need a new bladder.

BEN. Coming from you...

STEVEN. Be quick.

BEN. Jawohl!

STEVEN. Right, coffee break. Five minutes. Not a second longer.

BEN *walks out of the main door*.

BRUNO. Right. Hunt the Jaffas.

BRUNO *goes into the kitchen to get Jaffa Cakes. By now* MAGGIE *has come down from the ladder. She tries the light which goes on*.

DIANE. And there was light!

MAGGIE. Guess what, I've found a journalist who wants to interview you all.

CONNIE. Really?

MAGGIE. The brother of a friend at Jack's school who works for the *Gazette*. He said he'd do like a profile. Your favourite this and that, kind of thing. Nothing too… you know… but it could be fun.

DIANE. A bit of publicity might help.

CONNIE. Definitely. Steven, has it occurred to you a female voice might suit the lead on this.

STEVEN. What, as in… you?

CONNIE. Or Diane.

DIANE. Oh no, I'm happy where I am thanks.

STEVEN. I do think it suits Bruno's voice rather perfectly.

CONNIE. Everything seems to suit Bruno's voice rather perfectly.

MAGGIE. He does have a very nice voice.

CONNIE. But he's not the only one who can sing, is he?

MAGGIE. No. Far from it.

STEVEN. You yourself said we should play our strongest card so…

CONNIE. Oh so you think he's got the best voice.

STEVEN. I think he has the right voice. For this song.

CONNIE. Right MALE voice maybe. Funny though, you're in charge, you make the choices and somehow Bruno, a man, gets to sing the lead.

STEVEN. Because he has the right voice.

CONNIE. Says you.

DIANE. It wasn't a problem before.

MAGGIE. Maybe Connie should try it just to see…

STEVEN. No, we don't have time to experiment. Sorry.

CONNIE. Just thought I'd mention it.

BRUNO *enters*.

BRUNO (*entering*). The good news is I've found the Jaffas, the bad news is the cat's shat on the mat again.

STEVEN *and* DIANE. Oh no.

BRUNO. It must be Pavlovian. Every time the bulb goes the cat shits on the mat. Or the other way round.

DIANE. Has anyone come up with a name yet?

BRUNO. Ben's working on it.

CONNIE. Don't hold your breath.

BEN *comes back in*.

STEVEN. Sixty seconds.

CONNIE. What?

STEVEN. Left of the coffee break.

BEN. Up your Khyber.

STEVEN. It's a competition!

BEN. Up your other Khyber.

CONNIE. Ben!

STEVEN. Either we want to win or we don't.

MAGGIE. Who do you think's got the best voice in the group, Ben?

STEVEN. Maggie…

BEN. Easy. Me.

MAGGIE *laughs*.

MAGGIE. How did you two meet?

BEN. I won her in a raffle.

CONNIE. What do you want to know that for?

MAGGIE. You just seem so…

CONNIE (*beat*). Ill-matched?

MAGGIE. No! Not at all. Sometimes opposites attract, don't they.

CONNIE. Sometimes.

BEN. If you really want to know I saw her arse on a billboard.

CONNIE. Romantic, isn't it.

BEN. I was playing some tournament in Bournemouth. Made it through to the semis so I was feeling pretty chuffed. I was driving along and just outside the club I saw this huge poster. A woman sunbathing… or half a woman, bottom half, with a bottle of sun cream on her back. There was a pink bottle-shaped patch on her back. You remember? Anyway, I looked at this arse and I thought… if the top half's anything like as good as the bottom half, I want to meet this girl. Phoned up my agent, blah-de-blah, six o'clock that evening she was sitting in my Portakabin.

CONNIE. And nine months later Georgie was born.

MAGGIE. No!

BEN. Near enough.

CONNIE. I wasn't so much introduced as procured.

BEN. I went out the next day and played the game of my life. Thrashed some Aussie three sets to love.

CONNIE. Still managed to lose the final, though, didn't you.

BEN. I was exhausted by then.

MAGGIE. I think that's a lovely story.

BEN. It's true. Every word. Mind you, horses for courses, Diane… (*Re:* STEVEN.) if you'd seen his arse on a billboard you'd have run a mile, wouldn't you. Wouldn't she, Steven?

STEVEN. Better ask her. Time's up.

BEN. A three-minute mile.

DIANE. Not true.

STEVEN. People! We have exactly ten minutes and August 28th is looming. Maggie, would you mind doing us a huge favour and clearing up the cat mess, only…

MAGGIE. The catshit.

STEVEN. I know, I'm sorry it's just that we're rather fighting for time.

MAGGIE. No, no of course…

She goes across to the kitchen. A slight sense of unease. DIANE *notices she is put out.*

STEVEN. From the top…

CONNIE. As a matter of interest, who voted for this one?

STEVEN. More people than for any of the others.

BEN. Names?

STEVEN. It was a secret ballot. Are we going to sing this or not?

CONNIE. Secret to us.

STEVEN. Well obviously I had to know.

BEN. So it's just a stroke of luck that it was your favourite…

CONNIE. I didn't choose it.

BEN. Nor did I.

BRUNO. Nor me.

All eyes on DIANE.

DIANE. I did actually.

STEVEN. And so did I.

DIANE *follows* MAGGIE *into the kitchen.*

BRUNO. Which means that two people must have voted for one of the others as well.

STEVEN. Yes. And?

DIANE. Maggie? Are you okay?

BEN. So how come we've ended up doing this one?

MAGGIE. Yes, I'm fine.

STEVEN. Because this one got more second choice votes…

DIANE. Listen you don't have to clear this up…

BEN. I didn't vote for it first or second.

CONNIE. Me neither…

MAGGIE *crumbles*.

DIANE. Oh sweetheart. What's happened?

DIANE *puts her arm around* MAGGIE.

BEN. I don't suppose it's got anything to do with you trying to impress your would-be employers…

STEVEN (*losing his temper*). No! And at this rate we're not going to have ANYTHING to sing cos we'll have spent all our time arguing instead of rehearsing!

MAGGIE. They got it wrong. Can you believe it. They lost the sample or something. Some sort of mix-up. I had to go back in and have it taken again.

STEVEN. Diane!

DIANE. Oh no. And?

MAGGIE. It's malignant.

DIANE. I'm sorry.

MAGGIE. Grade two.

DIANE. What are they offering? Surgery?

STEVEN. Diane!

DIANE (*to* STEVEN). Just wait a second!

STEVEN. What's she doing?

DIANE. You can't sit in here. You mustn't.

MAGGIE. No I know. I just didn't want to spoil things. Everyone's so excited at the moment.

BEN. I knew it was a bad idea.

CONNIE. What?

BEN. This whole Talentfest thing.

CONNIE. It's not a bad idea. Why's it suddenly a bad idea?

DIANE. You're ill. You're not spoiling anything for anyone. And hiding isn't going to help…

CONNIE. Don't you start backing out now…

DIANE. Come on…

DIANE takes MAGGIE's hand and leads her back into the main room…

STEVEN. What's going on? We're trying to rehearse and you just bugger off into…

He sees MAGGIE's tears.

What's wrong?

DIANE. Maggie's had some bad news. They made a mistake.

CONNIE. Oh dear.

MAGGIE. Yes it's just… you know… same old…

She indicates her breast.

BEN. Oh no.

MAGGIE. Yes. A tumour after all I'm afraid. Quite a nasty one. Not that any of them are nice. They've had to take a bit from under my arm as well. Just in case. I'm sorry, I should have been straight with you.

DIANE. But it's treatable.

MAGGIE. Oh yes… Jan reckons once they've taken the lump out there's a good chance the chemo will do the trick. But you never quite know, do you…

DIANE. Jan?

MAGGIE. Jan Watson, she's my consultant.

DIANE. Oh she's good. I met her once actually. She's the best, they all said so.

STEVEN. I'm so sorry.

DIANE. You're in good hands.

MAGGIE. Just one of those things.

CONNIE. You should have said.

MAGGIE. I was going to. But then I thought… silly really but I thought you'd think I was only telling you so as you'd feel sorry for me.

DIANE. And what's wrong with that?

MAGGIE. I don't know. The truth is after last time… singing and that… it felt so good I didn't want you to feel you had to… include me so to speak… just because I was ill.

BRUNO. We've already included you. Long before all this came up.

BEN. Fifth Beatle.

MAGGIE. In the group I meant. Because I wouldn't want that. Not… you know… for that reason.

Pause.

Anyway, you've got work to do…

STEVEN. I think we'll call it a day. (*To the others.*) Don't you?

MAGGIE. I'm not sure when I'll see you all again. (*Getting tearful again.*) What with the surgery I don't know how I'll be feeling or…

DIANE. Maggie, we're here. We want to help. Don't we?

All agree.

And you're going to need help. With Jack, getting to the hospital, cooking… you are going to need help.

MAGGIE. I can't afford to pay for nannies and all that… I can hardly / afford –

BRUNO. What about family?

MAGGIE. My mum's coming to stay for a bit.

CONNIE. That's good.

DIANE. We will help you, time, money, whatever... won't we, Steven.

STEVEN *distracted*.

Steven?

STEVEN. Yes, sorry. What?

DIANE. We can bail Maggie out if she needs it.

STEVEN (*beat*). Yes of course. Absolutely.

MAGGIE (*tearful*). You're so kind. All of you.

DIANE. Come on, I'll see you out.

Goodbyes. She exits with MAGGIE. *Silence.*

BEN. Poor woman.

CONNIE. Poor Jack.

Pause.

BRUNO. We should ask her really, shouldn't we.

STEVEN. Ask her what?

BRUNO. To sing with us. For Talentfest.

CONNIE. You're not serious.

BRUNO. She's got a nice voice.

CONNIE. Ish. For a Welsh person you'd expect a lot better to be honest.

BRUNO. She's got cancer!

CONNIE. I know. And you're feeling sorry for her.

BRUNO. Yes I am. Aren't you?

CONNIE. Of course I am.

DIANE enters.

DIANE. We should ask her to join the group.

BRUNO. See?

CONNIE. She's not up to it.

BEN. It's exactly what she said she didn't want to happen.

DIANE. This could improve her chances of success.

BEN. Right so if we say no and she snuffs it, then it's our fault.

BRUNO. Hold on, she's not / going to die.

STEVEN. No one is dying.

BEN. For argument's sake.

DIANE. That's not what I said.

CONNIE. It kind of is actually. (*Beat.*) Could make it worse.

DIANE. How?

CONNIE. Singing is tiring. She's going to need all the energy she's got for the chemo and whatever else they chuck at her.

DIANE. She can always say no.

BRUNO. We're not going to be as good.

STEVEN. No.

DIANE. She's got a decent voice.

STEVEN. This is a competition.

CONNIE. If we are going to have any chance at all of getting through to the final we need to be at our best. Right? Don't get me wrong, I am gutted for her but I mean, do we want to win this or not?

BRUNO. She's going to expect it now.

STEVEN. Why?

BRUNO. She's done it once and we all told her how brilliant she was.

BEN. Yes but she knows.

BRUNO. That we were lying?

BEN. Not exactly lying.

DIANE. She was alright.

CONNIE. 'Alright'? We want good. We want bloody brilliant.

DIANE. What, like WE all are? It's a nice thing to do.

CONNIE. We're not doing 'nice' things, Diane. And like Steven said, we can't do it half-arsed. Do you realise what winning would mean?

DIANE. Connie… realistically…

CONNIE. What? You don't think we could go all the way? Let's not bother then. If we're not going to give it our best shot, let's not bother. You don't realise, do you. Any of you. Bruno, read them that bit you showed me… from the paper.

BRUNO. What? Oh…

BRUNO *fishes around in his bag and pulls out a paper clipping.*

CONNIE. You make your own luck, Maggie said as much, you make your own luck. Listen to this… (*To* BRUNO.) Read that bit out from before.

BRUNO (*reading.*) 'Previous winners Paul Potts…' this is *BGT* this is… 'Previous winners Paul Potts, Diversity, and Ashley and Pudsey changed their lives forever by applying for the show and this year, it could be your turn…'

CONNIE. There. In print. I know it's a long shot, but can you imagine? No more catshit. No more broken light bulbs. We'd be singing in theatres, recording studios, the Royal Variety even…

Disbelieving reaction.

You don't know! It's possible! You have to believe it's possible.

DIANE. We can still do all that and help her at the same time. How easy is it to write an extra part?

STEVEN. It's not hard. I think…

Pause. All eyes on STEVEN.

I think we should take a vote. Connie?

CONNIE. Whatever. I think you're all mad.

DIANE. Right. So, all those in favour of Maggie joining the group? Bruno?

BRUNO (*beat*). Yes.

DIANE. Me? Yes. Steven?

Pause. He doesn't answer.

STEVEN. Okay.

DIANE. Ben?

BEN. Can I abstain?

DIANE. No.

BEN. What, even if my life is at risk?

DIANE. No.

BEN. Bit harsh. (*Beat.*) Yes.

DIANE. Connie?

CONNIE. No.

DIANE. Right. Motion carried. Four to one.

BEN. Can we go home now?

DIANE. Assuming she WANTS to join.

STEVEN. I'm sure she does.

DIANE (*to* CONNIE). Sorry.

CONNIE. Great. AND I'm the baddie now.

BRUNO. Anyone in after us?

STEVEN. No.

BRUNO *closes the window.*

BRUNO. Who's for a quick one?

BEN. Champions League.

CONNIE. Not for me.

STEVEN. I've got to write a sixth harmony.

BRUNO. Diane?

STEVEN. She has book club.

DIANE (*to* STEVEN). It's too late for book club now. And I haven't read it anyway. (*To* BRUNO.) Why not?

She goes round collecting coffee cups.

BEN. Had a think about the stamps?

STEVEN. What?

BEN. The stamps.

STEVEN. Oh yes. I have as a matter of fact. I'm interested.

BEN. Great. Both or just the one?

STEVEN. Just the one I think.

DIANE. I can lock up if you like.

BEN. I'll bring it in so you can have a look.

CONNIE. What stamps?

STEVEN. Your husband is selling me a stamp.

CONNIE. Stamps now, is it?

BEN. Diversification. Look it up.

STEVEN. Actually, Diane, I think I will come. The harmonies can wait.

DIANE (*beat*). For a drink?

STEVEN. Yes.

DIANE. Right. Great.

BRUNO. Great.

STEVEN (*to* BRUNO). We'll see you in there.

BRUNO *goes out.*

CONNIE. I can GIVE you a stamp if you want.

STEVEN (*beat*). Sorry?

CONNIE. I said I can give you a stamp.

STEVEN. No it's a special one.

CONNIE. Oh I see. How much?

STEVEN. Eight hundred pounds.

CONNIE. Eight hundr… For one stamp!

BEN. It's special.

CONNIE. What, special delivery by hand to New Zealand.

BEN. Don't / be…

CONNIE. It'll probably have something wrong with it and all.

BEN. It does.

CONNIE. Knew it. At least he's honest.

BEN (*to* STEVE). Welcome to my world.

> BEN *and* CONNIE *exit.* STEVEN *and* DIANE *finish tidying up.*

DIANE. Ready?

STEVEN. No. There's something I need to say.

> *Pause.*

DIANE. What?

> STEVEN *goes to the double doors and opens them to check that everyone has left. He returns. Pause.* DIANE *on tenterhooks.*

STEVEN. This is not easy.

DIANE. For God's sake just say it.

STEVEN. I don't actually have any concrete evidence per se… but I've had a bit of a metaphorical and a literal light-bulb moment.

DIANE. Steven…

STEVEN. You see I know only too well, as do you, what happens when you have a biopsy from that particular area of the body.

DIANE (*relieved*). What?

STEVEN. You wouldn't be able to lift your arm above your shoulder, not for a couple of weeks at least. It's that painful. Someone has to help you dress, wash your hair, move things down from the cupboards. Remember?

DIANE. Of course.

STEVEN. The idea that Maggie would be able to climb up a ladder and change a light bulb… with her arm up here. Impossible.

DIANE. Right. So what are you saying, you think she's lying?

STEVEN. As I say, I know as evidence goes it's not conclusive.

DIANE. To put it mildly.

STEVEN. But from the second she walked into our rehearsal that very first day. I just got a / strange…

DIANE. We're not clones, you know. Not all operations are the same.

STEVEN. I know but when you said they'd made a mistake, it suddenly kind of made sense. Or rather it stopped making sense. I mean they don't 'make mistakes'…

DIANE. Of course they do, people have had the wrong leg amputated!

STEVEN. All that stuff about her second husband… and the wedding and… even her son, I've never seen Jack. Not once. No one has. Or her mother for that matter. Maggie's been in the village nearly three months.

DIANE. That is crazy! You really think she would invent a child.

STEVEN. I'm not / saying…

DIANE. Why?

STEVEN. …she has. I'm just saying that there is something odd about her.

DIANE. You are saying that she's a liar. And that in spite of everything that we know about her, she is lying about her illness. Yes?

STEVEN. What do we know about her? Only what she's told us.

DIANE. Why would she lie about something like that?

STEVEN. I don't know. Perhaps she's ill in a different way. In the grip / of some obsessive…

DIANE. Steven!

STEVEN. Calm down.

DIANE. If someone said to you, when you were at your most vulnerable, trying to deal with all the shit you have to deal with when you're told you have cancer, if someone accused you of lying / about it…

STEVEN. I haven't accused her.

DIANE. It would finish you off. There and then. It's about the most insulting, / insensitive…

STEVEN. I haven't accused her.

DIANE. To her face maybe not but behind her back. It's disgusting. She has cancer.

STEVEN. You don't know that.

DIANE. I DO know that. She's not lying!

STEVEN. I was a schoolmaster for nearly forty years and I think I have a pretty good idea when someone is deceiving me.

Silence.

DIANE. So what are you going to do?

STEVEN. I wasn't intending to do anything.

DIANE. Why not? If that's what you think. Confront her. Say something. Write something. Put your money where your mouth is.

STEVEN. Is that what you think I should do?

DIANE. Or maybe you're not so sure as you make out.

STEVEN. Is that what you want me to do?

DIANE. No!

STEVEN. Then I won't.

Pause.

We'd better get out of here. We don't want to keep Bruno waiting.

They exit. Blackout.

End of Act One.

ACT TWO

Lights up on MAGGIE *in the same position as her opening monologue.*

MAGGIE. 'Invisible glue' my dad used to call it. He used to say about football hooligans. 'Meet them on their own in the street or the post office wherever, they'll be nice as pie but put them altogether… Like a pack of wolves.' And he was right. If I was going to point the finger at one person… it would have to be Steven. He was the ringleader if you like. Though I have to say I rather took to him at first. He seemed kind. Interested. But it turned out it was all a front. He was thinking things the whole time. Really nasty things. She was just as bad, the wife. Even though oddly enough she was the one who first invited me to sing. I never asked. She was very unhappy. I could tell. I remember seeing her once. Stood outside the chemist she was, staring at this baby in a pram. Just staring. As if she was thinking about taking it. Like one of them madwomen you see on the telly. That would explain a lot.

Lights up on the village hall. CONNIE, BEN *and* STEVEN *at the piano. There is a small PA set up* (*desk with two speakers*) *but no mics.*

BEN. She's pregnant!?

STEVEN *and* CONNIE. No!

MAGGIE (*still to audience*). Jealous, see.

CONNIE. Steven's agreed to try for another.

MAGGIE (*to audience*). Of my Jack.

STEVEN. How did you know?

CONNIE. She phoned me yesterday.

BEN. Sprog number five.

STEVEN. In theory yes.

CONNIE. I knew she'd win you round.

STEVEN. Did you? How?

CONNIE. Because underneath it all you're a big softie.

BEN (*to* CONNIE). How did you know she even wanted one?

CONNIE. Women talk to each other! The thing is, Steven... for us women it's not like an idea. Something you quite fancy. It's more physical. More like a hunger. And you don't always know if and when you're going to be hungry. Doesn't matter if she didn't want it ten years ago, she does now.

BEN. You'll have your own football team soon...

STEVEN. Well... it's not altogether straightforward as it happens. Being older.

CONNIE. Oh?

STEVEN. Not... no.

Pause.

I'm not sure I really want to / go into any...

CONNIE. Oh go on. You're amongst friends.

STEVEN. Well. Apparently if you imagine a large pool.

CONNIE. A large what?

STEVEN. Pool.

CONNIE. Right.

STEVEN. Swimming pool.

CONNIE. Like an infinity pool.

STEVEN. Any old pool.

BEN. It's a metaphor, for God's sake.

CONNIE. Alright, alright.

STEVEN. Yes. And then imagine a handful of not very good swimmers, swimmers with one arm say... or one leg... NO legs for that matter... all of whom are a little bit tired.

Clearly any kind of race to a specific point in that pool is going to be compromised to say the least. Well apparently that's kind of what my… that's my situation.

CONNIE. Riiight.

DIANE *comes in*.

DIANE. Hi.

BEN (*giving her a hug*). Congratulations.

DIANE. Oh thank you! I am so excited. I didn't sleep a wink last night.

BEN. Oi, oi. (*To* STEVEN.) Quick off the mark.

DIANE. How much have you… what have you been talking about?

BEN. Sperm.

DIANE. Oh right.

BEN. I think. Either that or the Paralympics.

STEVEN. I was just explaining that once… sperm… reaches a certain vintage, unlike wine with the possible exception of Beaujolais, it deteriorates. In quality and quantity.

DIANE. Yes. And taste.

BEN. Steady!

DIANE. The Beaujolais. I meant the Beaujolais.

BEN. You won't get pregnant like that I'm telling you.

DIANE. I really did mean the Beaujolais.

CONNIE. So does that mean… what does that mean?

DIANE. It might mean we'd have to find a donor.

CONNIE. Oh right.

STEVEN. Depending on the test results.

BEN. So do you just go to some kind of data bank, type in the details, and up pops a name?

DIANE. More or less yes.

CONNIE. What details?

BEN. Depends what kind of baby you want.

STEVEN. You choose... Eyes, hair.

BEN. You definitely want them.

STEVEN. Ethnicity.

BEN. So if you want short, fat and good at hockey...

DIANE. In fact...

CONNIE. Don't be silly.

BEN. You can!

CONNIE. Who's going to want short, fat and good at hockey!

BEN. Takes all sorts.

DIANE. It rather smacks of eugenics to me. I'd be happy whatever the ethnicity.

CONNIE. Would you?

BEN. Brave.

STEVEN. I'm just not sure it would be fair. On the baby.

DIANE. Only that's a teeny bit racist.

STEVEN. It's concern for the baby's welfare. He or she will need to feel they belong.

DIANE. Then we'll do everything we can to help them belong.

CONNIE. Oh you'll work it out. I'm sure you will.

STEVEN. If we don't go bankrupt first.

DIANE. It's a question of numbers in the end. No matter how old you are. The more quality eggs, the more quality sperm, the better your chances. But we don't have time to faff around designing our ideal child we just need to... get on with it!

Pause.

STEVEN. It's not straightforward but I will do whatever it takes for Diane to have a baby.

BEN. Because he loves you.

STEVEN. Yes actually. Because I love her.

CONNIE. Ah. I think I'm going to cry.

BEN. Oh God. Listen if push comes to shove you can have one of ours.

CONNIE. Ben!

BEN. One of the twins obviously…

CONNIE. Stop it!

BRUNO (*off*). Delivery!

DIANE. Shh.

BEN. Mate's rates.

BRUNO (*off*). Any spare hands?

STEVEN. Coming… Do you mind if we keep this strictly 'entre nous'?

DIANE. Yes. Really.

CONNIE. Of course. Of course.

STEVEN *gets up and goes out.*

DIANE. So when are you two moving?

CONNIE. Ha! When are we moving, Ben?

BEN. When are you winning the lottery?

STEVEN *and* BRUNO *enter carrying microphone stands and cables.* MAGGIE *follows carrying an armful of microphones.*

Any more?

BRUNO. That's the lot.

STEVEN. Over here I think.

MAGGIE. What about these mics?

BEN. Should you be carrying those?

BEN *relieves* MAGGIE *of the mics.*

MAGGIE. Oh thanks. I was terrified I was going to drop them.

STEVEN. Let's get one of them working so we can brush up on our microphone technique.

STEVEN *and* BEN *start to assemble the mics and stands.* BRUNO *connects them to the desk.*

BRUNO. We still haven't got a name. They've been asking.

DIANE. Ben?

BEN. How about: 'The Humming Birds'.

BRUNO. That's pretty good.

MAGGIE. I like that.

CONNIE. Humming birds don't sing.

BEN. Course they do. All birds sing.

CONNIE. No they don't.

MAGGIE. Catchy.

BEN. Name me one bird that doesn't sing.

CONNIE. A duck.

BEN. Oh for / God's…

CONNIE. They quack. If you hadn't noticed.

DIANE. And humming birds hum.

CONNIE. Otherwise / great.

BEN. Alright, alright. The Nightingales.

MAGGIE. Oh even better.

DIANE. I like that.

STEVEN. We all like that?

DIANE *and* CONNIE. Perfect. / Okay.

STEVEN. The Nightingales it is.

BRUNO. Nice one, Ben.

STEVEN. Found your metier at last.

BRUNO. Say something, will you, Maggie.

MAGGIE. I'm sorry?

BRUNO. Into the mic.

MAGGIE. Oh right.

> *She goes to the mic. At first it is not working.*

You know I've never held one of these before let alone sung into one. When I was in junior school…

> *The mic comes on.*

Oh my God is that me… loud or what. Yeah I used to stand on the desk with Jackie Bevan and we'd mime to *Top of the Pops* using tennis rackets as microphones. Now here I am with the real thing. Makes you feel like Elvis, doesn't it.

BRUNO. Best not to touch it.

MAGGIE. How close to the mic do we need to be?

BRUNO. About four inches?

MAGGIE. Four inches. How far is that?

BEN. Ask Diane. She'll tell you.

STEVEN. What the hell is that supposed to mean?

> *A beat. Then* STEVEN *walks out.*

What's up with him?

DIANE. He's a bit… (*Beat.*) He didn't get the St Michael's job.

CONNIE. Oh no.

DIANE. Pipped at the post for the third time in a year. By someone younger. Again. And yet they claimed they wanted someone with more experience.

MAGGIE. That's unfair, isn't it. A man with Steven's background. They'd be lucky to get him.

BRUNO. Alright, Maggie?

MAGGIE. I hope so.

BRUNO. Anyone else?

DIANE *goes out after* STEVEN.

CONNIE. Bruno, do we move our arm out during the second verse or the third?

BEN. Second.

BRUNO. Third!

BEN. See!

BRUNO. And a nice smooth movement.

BEN (*on* MIKE). Hello, hello, hello. Mary had a little lamb.

CONNIE. Which arm again?

BEN. She also had a bear.

BRUNO. If you're on the right, your right arm…

BEN. I've often seen her little lamb.

CONNIE. I swear to God I married a five-year-old. Sorry, Bruno, which arm?

BRUNO. For you it's your left.

MAGGIE *laughs. They look at her. She points at* BEN.

MAGGIE. I've only just got it.

CONNIE (*to* BEN). Move over, let me have a go…

She moves to the mic.

(*Beat.*) Can't think of anything to say now.

BEN. That's a first.

CONNIE. One two one two…

BEN. She gets stuck after that.

STEVEN *and* DIANE *return.*

BRUNO. Don't be scared of the microphone. Speak straight into it, not across it.

CONNIE. Right. (*On mic.*) Sorry to hear about the St Michael's job, Steven.

BRUNO. That's it…

BEN. Yeah.

STEVEN. Oh I'm not that fussed to be honest. Too far away anyway. Probably a blessing in disguise.

BRUNO. Any other takers?

MAGGIE. I wouldn't mind another…

She stops and starts breathing heavily. She sits down.

Oh dear.

BEN. What's up?

MAGGIE. I don't suppose I could have a glass of water, could I?

DIANE. Of course.

DIANE *goes to the kitchen.*

MAGGIE. I'm a bit short of breath all of a sudden…

BEN. Do you need to lie down?

MAGGIE. No I'll be fine. Really. Just catches up with you sometimes, that's all.

STEVEN. Perhaps you shouldn't have carried those mics so soon after surgery.

MAGGIE. Yeah you're probably right.

DIANE (*entering*). They weren't that heavy.

MAGGIE. No more chemo though. For three weeks! Jan helped me plan it that way, bless her. (*Takes the water.*) Look at me, being waited on hand and foot. You here, Mum at home. I feel like Lady Muck.

DIANE. I remembered something yesterday which I thought might help you.

MAGGIE. Oh yes?

DIANE. It sounds ridiculous but… my sister Carol had breast cancer… and…

MAGGIE. Your sister?

DIANE. Yes.

MAGGIE. Oh I'm sorry...

DIANE. It actually did help her in some way. She named her breasts.

MAGGIE. She did what?

DIANE. She named them. Bonnie and Clyde.

BEN. She named her breasts after two American gangsters? Which was which?

CONNIE. Does it matter?

DIANE. It helped her... connect with them somehow. That's what she said anyway.

MAGGIE. Right.

DIANE. It might help you. You never know.

BEN. Laurel and Hardy? Little and Large?

CONNIE. Ben!

MAGGIE. No it's fine. I need to laugh. Little and Large.

CONNIE. I never even knew you had a sister.

STEVEN. Twin.

BEN. Really?

MAGGIE. Was she alright in the end?

DIANE. Carol? Yes. Yes, full recovery.

MAGGIE. Oh good.

STEVEN (*beat*). How's Jack by the way?

MAGGIE. Oh he's great thanks.

STEVEN. You should bring him in one day.

MAGGIE. Do you think so?

STEVEN. Yes, why not? A chance to hear his mum singing.

MAGGIE. I don't know.

STEVEN. I hope he's coming to Leeds.

MAGGIE. Yes maybe.

A look between DIANE *and* STEVEN.

STEVEN (*beat*). Right. Five days, everybody!

Snap blackout.

Lights up on BEN *and* CONNIE *sitting on chairs.* CONNIE *is wearing a rather eye-catching jacket.*

CONNIE. Are you not taking photos? I thought you might have had a photographer.

BEN (*laughing*). Told you. Only went and put her glad rags on.

CONNIE. No, no don't worry. So… Purple. Always has been. Ever since I was a little girl. Seven… don't me ask me why. Shirley Bassey. 'Goldfinger'… sends shivers up my spine every time I hear it. What does the group…? Oh goodness. It's… it's… what's that word when you… oh what's that word…

BEN. Give us a clue.

CONNIE. Oh you know… it means…

BEN. It means we could be here a long time.

CONNIE. You know… something that calms you down…

BEN. Gin and tonic.

CONNIE. No.

BEN. Tranquilliser.

CONNIE. No! It's on the tip of my tongue…

BEN. Homeopathic tranquilliser…

CONNIE. I want to say arthritic…

BEN. What!

CONNIE. Cathartic! That's it. It's cathartic. And it's fun. Ambition? To wrap my legs round Simon Cowell.

BEN. Steady!

CONNIE. I'm joking.

BEN. He's a young lad.

CONNIE. Sorry. Don't print that, will you. Promise?

BEN. Better not.

CONNIE. I tell you what, did you ever see that film *Sliding Doors*? I love that film. It's about this woman who's about to get on a train and in one version… she gets on, goes home and finds her boyfriend in bed with another woman but in another version… cos you get to see both… in the other version the doors close just before she gets on, so she has to wait and catch the next train, which means that by the time she gets home the other woman has left so she never finds out. See what I mean? So it's like if little things hadn't happened. If you hadn't got up ten minutes late or… you hadn't answered the phone or whatever… there are all these other lives we might have lived. And yet you end up stuck with just the one. (*Beat.*) I think I'd like to be one of those Buddhists or Hindus is it… where they get to come back as something else. Mind you knowing my luck I'd be a stick insect or something and I'd just get trodden on. (*Beat.*) It's not an ambition as such cos it's not possible is it but… yes, it would be nice to have another go.

BEN. Deep.

CONNIE. Better deep than shallow. Your turn. Favourite number.

BEN. Two thousand four hundred and thirty-eight.

CONNIE *dismissive*.

What? Alright, two and a half.

CONNIE. Be sensible just for once.

BEN. Next? Favourite colour… (*Thinks.*) What do you want to know that for anyway?

CONNIE. Doesn't matter.

BEN. Haven't got one really.

CONNIE. Ben! Don't be difficult, just choose one.

BEN. I don't have one.

CONNIE. Everyone has a favourite colour.

BEN. I don't.

CONNIE (*spelling it out*). Everyone has a favourite colour.

BEN. Everyone except me.

CONNIE. You must have one.

BEN. Why? They're all the same to me. They're just colours.

CONNIE. Sorry about this. (*To* BEN.) Just say a colour.

BEN. You say one since it's / so important –

CONNIE. But it won't be your favourite, will it. Christ! It's not like it's hard. It's not like it's… brain science.

BEN. Brain science! What's that? Do you by any chance mean rocket science? Or brain surgery. I think you'll find it's one or the other. Brain science. You've got to get that in.

CONNIE. I'm just saying it's not hard.

BEN. No, you're right, it's not rocket surgery.

CONNIE. Oh for goodness' / sake.

BEN. But the fact is I don't have one. If it's an apple I like it to be green. If it's a banana I like it / to be yellow…

CONNIE. We're not talking about fruit. What are you talking about fruit for?

BEN. Why am I not allowed not to have a favourite colour?!

Silence. CONNIE *gives up.*

Alright then, alright… grey.

CONNIE. Oh for God's sake!

BEN. What now?

CONNIE. Grey is not a colour.

BEN. Grey is not… What planet are you from? What is it if it's not a colour?!

CONNIE. It's not a proper colour.

BEN. Not a / proper…

CONNIE. Just do the boy a favour and choose a colour with some fucking colour in it!

She gets up and goes. Silence.

BEN. Sorry about that. Just put whatever colour you want. Singer? Noel Gallagher. Tells it how it is. The group? Keeps Connie happy. Not. I don't know… a bit of fun. A few laughs even. Used to be anyway. Ambition? Staying alive. There. Any more? Favourite food? No? Arsenic for the record. Not for me though. Right. Can I go?

Blackout on BEN.

Lights come up on the kitchen and hall. DIANE *and* BRUNO *are lying side by side on the table, post-coital. In the hall,* DIANE's *scarf is on the piano.*

BRUNO. I was woken up by Mum at about four o'clock this morning. All dressed up with her handbag and ready to go out. I asked her where she was going and she said her son was coming to pick her up. And I said 'Mum, I'm your son.' She said 'Really? What's your name?' And I said 'Bruno.' And she laughed and said 'That's amazing'. I asked why and she said because she had a son called Bruno as well. (*Beat.*) She doesn't even know who I am any more.

DIANE. I'm sorry.

Pause. She kisses him.

BRUNO. I love you. (*Beat.*) I've been thinking.

DIANE. Yes?

BRUNO. About us.

DIANE. Right.

BRUNO. And… don't… you know, panic or anything just… hear me out. There's a spare room in Mum's house. It used to be hers but it's basically empty now. I was thinking I could turn it into a room for us. I don't just mean for... this, I mean where you could actually come and stay and spend time. And live.

DIANE. Live? You mean leave Steven and move in with you?

BRUNO. Well not LEAVE Steven but... Jesus, Diane, this is 2018, we don't have to live in neat little coupledom any more, there are all sorts of combinations and arrangements that could work if people just had the balls to try them and... don't you think? I have to keep saying it... I love you. I've never felt like this before in my life, I can't help it, it's like some exciting, dangerous illness which has spread to every...

He stops suddenly. they both freeze. STEVEN enters the hall. He has a quick look round, sees it is empty and is about to go when he sees DIANE's scarf on the piano. He stares at it for a moment, then turns and clocks the closed kitchen door. BRUNO and DIANE still frozen. STEVEN walks slowly towards the kitchen. He puts his hand on the doorhandle as if to go in. All three frozen. He ponders for a moment but decides not to turn the handle. He listens for a moment... and then turns and walks back out of the hall.

Who was that?

DIANE. Caretaker.

BRUNO. How do you know?

DIANE. Must have been. He's got the only other key.

BRUNO. Jesus. That wasn't Steven...

DIANE. No.

BRUNO. Only ever since he came to the pub.

DIANE. That was just... a whim.

BRUNO. Twice, Diane. He has come for a drink twice now.

DIANE. Not recently.

BRUNO. Whims are one-offs, they don't happen twice in a row.

DIANE. You think he wouldn't have said something? He hasn't got a key.

BRUNO. Was the door definitely locked?

DIANE. Yes.

BRUNO. You're sure.

DIANE. Yes.

BRUNO. Just check it, will you. For my sake.

DIANE. Bruno…

BRUNO. Please…

> DIANE *goes nervously into the hall and out to the main door. She comes back.*

DIANE. It's okay. It's locked. It must have been the caretaker. I think we'd better leave though…

> *She stops. She stares at her scarf on the stool.*

BRUNO. Diane?

> *She doesn't answer.*

Diane?

> *He enters. She is still staring.*

What is it?

DIANE. Nothing. It's fine. It's all fine.

> *Blackout.*

> *Lights up on the hall. A buzz of excitement.* CONNIE *is centre stage wearing an eye-grabbing black-and-red dress.* MAGGIE *stands behind her, sewing her in.* BEN *watches.*

CONNIE. The moment of truth.

MAGGIE. Don't. I'm all jelly inside as it is.

CONNIE *(re: dress)*. I meant this.

BEN. I thought we were getting dressed there.

CONNIE. Won't be time. Ouch!

MAGGIE. Sorry! Sorry!

CONNIE. Or space.

MAGGIE. Hold still a minute. Breathe in.

CONNIE. I couldn't get to sleep last night. I was doing all the moves in bed. Wrong. And THEN… then I dreamt that Louis Walsh and… what's that politician…

BEN. Here we go.

CONNIE.…who danced…

BEN. Vince Cable.

CONNIE. No the OTHER one… with the wife…

BEN. Oh THAT one.

CONNIE.…funny little legs…

BEN. Ann Widdicombe.

CONNIE. No.

BEN. Balls.

CONNIE. Yes! That's the one. I was singing my heart out and when I looked round Louis Walsh and Ed Balls were my backing vocalists.

BEN. That's not a dream, it's a nightmare. Where's Steven?

STEVEN *and* DIANE *enter.* STEVEN *is carrying a bag.*

DIANE. Steven is here. (*Sees* CONNIE.) Wow!

STEVEN. Ooh. Goodness.

CONNIE. What do you think? Not too much?

BEN. Too little if you ask me.

DIANE. You look gorgeous.

MAGGIE. Doesn't she. There. All done.

DIANE. Are you going to be alright in that for six hours?

CONNIE. Just watch me.

BRUNO *enters carrying a bag.*

BRUNO. It's real. It's happening. And it's... (*Sees* CONNIE.) Whoa! I didn't know Liz Taylor had joined the group.

CONNIE. Stop it! You know the last time I wore this? Seventeen years ago. I've not worn it since. Had to make the odd alteration mind.

BRUNO. In or out?

CONNIE. Mr Smoothie.

BRUNO. Hey. Check out the socks.

He lifts his trousers to reveal red socks. Appreciation all round.

DIANE. Nice.

BEN. Sexy or what.

CONNIE. What's your red, Steven?

STEVEN. Handkerchief. Top pocket.

CONNIE. Oh very classy.

STEVEN. So are you not bringing Jack, Maggie?

MAGGIE. No. No I thought in the end I wouldn't. It's a bit late for him to be honest. I've sorted out a sleepover.

DIANE *and* STEVEN *share a look.*

STEVEN. What about your mum?

MAGGIE. What about her?

STEVEN. Would she like a lift?

MAGGIE. Oh, she's making her own way, thanks. Once she's got Jack sorted. He's a bit all over the place. You can imagine, what with everything else he's had to deal with.

DIANE. Of course.

CONNIE. Any idea how many people are coming?

DIANE. They're sold out.

CONNIE. No!

DIANE. Have been for weeks.

CONNIE. Do you think Louis Walsh will be there?

BEN. No chance.

CONNIE. I expect he'll be there at Blackpool.

BEN. Unlike us.

CONNIE. Don't pour cold water on everything. Not today of all days.

BEN. You alright, Maggie?

MAGGIE. Yes! Just a bit hot. Excitement probably. Reminds me of when I got married. Running around like a headless chicken trying to organise everything.

DIANE. You'll be fine.

MAGGIE. Though I did get to meet the Queen.

BEN. You what!

STEVEN. The Queen came to your wedding?

MAGGIE. No, no. Now that would have been something. No but what it was I was working at the local hospital at the time and they were building a new wing and they invited Her Majesty to open it. We all had to line up when she came in, you know like they do at Wimbledon, and she walked along nodding at all of us. And SOMEONE… to this day I don't know who… but someone had told her I was getting married. And she stopped in front of me, looked me in the eye and congratulated me there and then.

DIANE. What did you say?

MAGGIE. I didn't say a word. I couldn't. I was so choked up.

STEVEN. I bet you were.

CONNIE *opens her bag*.

BEN. What are you doing? I've just spent half the morning trying to close it.

CONNIE. I've got Smints here if anyone needs them.

BEN. Connie...

CONNIE. No one's going to win with halitosis are they...

She pulls out a jacket.

What are you bringing this for? You are not wearing that.

BEN. Why not?

CONNIE. You are not / wearing that.

BEN. It's not a fashion show.

CONNIE. It's got holes in it.

BEN. Paid extra for those.

CONNIE. Do you want to win? Cos some of us do and I can tell you you're not wearing that. What's your red?

BEN. Underpants.

CONNIE. Underpants! Who's going to see those?

BEN. Might get lucky.

MAGGIE. I think it looks alright.

CONNIE. No it doesn't, Maggie. It looks bloody awful.

STEVEN. Something that expresses your personality. Is the official brief.

CONNIE. Yeah that's the problem. (*To* BEN.) I wish for one second, just one second you would take this seriously!

MAGGIE *suddenly stands up and heads for the door.*

STEVEN. Maggie?

She exits. STEVEN *follows* MAGGIE *out.*

BEN. She shouldn't have done this. It's too much for her.

CONNIE. What I said in the first place.

BEN. It's supposed to be helping her.

DIANE. How do you know it's not?

STEVEN *comes back in.*

STEVEN (*to* DIANE). I think she's being sick. Nerves I expect.

DIANE. Or chemo.

DIANE goes out.

CONNIE. Now, Steven…

She checks the door is closed.

I read online… they sometimes like to have a little chat.

STEVEN. Who?

CONNIE. The judges. Which, if it happens, is a good thing as it means they're interested.

STEVEN. Yes don't worry, the thought / had crossed…

CONNIE. I don't think it should be you.

STEVEN. Why not?

CONNIE. If you don't mind my saying. I think you're a bit posh.

STEVEN. Right.

CONNIE. I think it should be Maggie.

STEVEN. Maggie?

CONNIE. Yes.

STEVEN. Why? She's not the most… articulate person.

BEN. She's genuine.

CONNIE. I think she's very articulate. She doesn't use long words if that's what you mean.

BRUNO. Hasn't she got enough to worry about?

CONNIE. Well why should it be Steven? Just cos he went to Cambridge or wherever…

BEN. I'll do it if you want.

CONNIE. Ha!

BRUNO. He has been running the group for some time…

CONNIE. The thing is… we need to tell them, don't we. I mean it would be stupid not to.

STEVEN. What?

CONNIE. About Maggie. Being ill.

BRUNO. Do we?

CONNIE. Even better if she does it herself.

BEN *reacts*.

What? You know as well as I do if you've got a dying granny or a disabled child or whatever, they're all over you. I don't know why you're acting so shocked. As if it's not true.

BRUNO. That's pretty...

CONNIE. Like it or not, it's the way it works. It's not like we've given her cancer on purpose just to improve our chances of winning.

BRUNO. Even so.

CONNIE. She'll be fine with it.

BEN. At this rate they won't need telling.

CONNIE. We can't NOT tell them. It's not fair on her, is it. If she's under par, they need to know why. And like I said, it could help us.

BEN. What do you want to do, hang a sign round her neck?

CONNIE. Oh don't be / stupid...

STEVEN. How about asking her? She might not want them to know.

CONNIE. If you like.

MAGGIE *comes back in with* DIANE.

Everything okay?

MAGGIE. Sorry about that. It's normal, it is. My body thinks it's being poisoned.

DIANE. Which it is.

BEN. So how are we travelling?

STEVEN. We'll take the bags.

BEN. You coming with us, Maggie?

MAGGIE. If it's alright / with you.

STEVEN. No I think it's better if we take Maggie. (*Beat.*) Bruno could use the extra legroom I'm sure…

BRUNO. Me?

STEVEN. Unless there's someone else called Bruno I don't know about.

BRUNO (*beat*). Fine.

STEVEN. You alright with that, Maggie?

MAGGIE. I'm happy whichever way.

BRUNO. What about Maggie's Jack?

STEVEN. He's not coming.

BRUNO. Oh that's a shame. I saw him the other day.

MAGGIE. Did you?

BRUNO. In the Co-op.

STEVEN *looks at him.*

What?

STEVEN. Nothing.

BRUNO. He doesn't half look like you.

MAGGIE. Oh I know. Poor thing. As if he didn't have enough on his plate. Hope he was polite.

BRUNO. He was lovely.

MAGGIE. You know I'll tell you something. The one thing I've learned from all this silly business… is that I'm not afraid of death. Or dying. Not that I'm going to… but if I was… that doesn't worry me in the least. Not even… things getting worse. Pain whatever. No the only thing that I lose sleep about is Jack. (*Suddenly very emotional.*) And how he would cope.

DIANE *and* STEVEN *exchange looks.* DIANE *goes over and puts her arm around her.*

DIANE. You're going to be fine. And so is Jack.

MAGGIE. I know.

CONNIE. We were just saying actually we think it might be a good idea to tell the judges about your illness.

MAGGIE. Really?

CONNIE. Yes, so they understand.

DIANE. Is that a good idea?

MAGGIE. They won't disqualify us or anything.

BRUNO. No of course not, why would they.

MAGGIE. I don't know I…

CONNIE. If anything it would make them like us more.

MAGGIE. Oh well, we want that, don't we.

DIANE. Are you sure?

MAGGIE. Yes. If it helps, why not?

Pause.

CONNIE. So are we all agreed then?

Awkward half-hearted agreement.

Do you want to tell them yourself or would you rather one of us did it?

MAGGIE. I think maybe it's best coming from someone else. I'd feel a bit… you know. Like I was spoiling things.

CONNIE. Not at all…

DIANE. Connie, if she's not keen…

MAGGIE. I'm not really.

CONNIE. Fine. Bruno then. If Bruno did the chat then he could bring it up.

BRUNO. Me?

CONNIE. You could work it in, couldn't you?

BRUNO. Why me?

CONNIE. The thing is we are a bit rural, aren't we, a bit…
I think we need a broader appeal. Which you can do.

BRUNO. How exactly do I broaden the appeal?

CONNIE. You know… you give us a bit of… I don't know…
urban edge.

BRUNO. Do I?

CONNIE. Well obviously. You're young… or younger.

BRUNO. Yes.

CONNIE. And you're black.

BRUNO. Perfect. So young and black equals urban edge.

CONNIE. I'm not saying it's true.

BRUNO. No, it's not. And they'll know that the second I open
my middle-class mouth.

BEN. Why do we want 'urban edge'? This is Tapley, for God's
sake! Why pretend to be something that we're not?

BRUNO. I could do a bit of breakdancing in the middle of the
song. Wear a baseball cap?

CONNIE. It's nothing personal, Bruno, I don't normally even
think of you as being black.

BRUNO. Stop. Now.

CONNIE. To me we're all the same colour.

BEN. But we're not.

BRUNO. No. Think of me as black.

CONNIE. Why?

BRUNO. Because I fucking am!

CONNIE. Easy!

STEVEN. Bloody hell, there's no winning is there.

BRUNO. What!

STEVEN. Calm down, Bruno!

BRUNO. You calm down! What's wrong with you people?

STEVEN. US people?

Silence.

BRUNO. Right. So am I doing this talk or what? Steven, if you want / to –

STEVEN. No, no. The consensus now seems to be that you're the man for the job. You clearly have the gift of the gab and you appeal to a wide demographic or so it would seem so... All yours.

BRUNO. Fine.

CONNIE. Sorted.

An awkward atmosphere. The lights fade on the hall as everyone goes about their preparations. MAGGIE *steps into a spotlight.*

MAGGIE. It was just after that that I realised. Sitting in Steven's car on the way up to Leeds. Imagining the audience. I didn't say anything at the time because they were so hyped up. Excited I suppose. I was. I say excited, but the truth is I was more terrified. See it only occurred to me then that the last time I'd stood up in front of a large crowd of people was at my dad's funeral. My mother had asked me to sing a song. A lullaby really, the same one Dad used to sing to get me to sleep. (*Sings.*) 'Huna, blentyn, ar fy mynwes, Clyd a chynnes ydyw hon...' And of course I agreed because I wanted to please her. And him. But I was only ten and when it came to it... when I saw all those people sat in front of me. Staring. And what with the coffin and whatnot.

Pause.

I think she was disappointed. I know she was. (*Beat.*) Funny though, isn't it, how these things just pop into your head. And once they're there, you can't get rid of them for love nor money.

Blackout on MAGGIE. *Immediately the growing sound of an expectant audience. It should feel like a sizeable crowd. Suddenly six spotlights appear on stage.* CONNIE, BEN,

STEVEN, DIANE *and* BRUNO *step into the spotlights all dressed to the nines. Wild applause and then the sound of the audience quietens till you could hear a pin drop.* STEVEN *takes out a tuning fork. He taps it on his knee and holds it up to his microphone. A loud 'A' resonates. He raises his hands and after a moment of letting the sound fade away conducts them into the song. They start singing 'You Raise Me Up'. It starts off really well and we might think they are going to triumph, but after a while nerves get the better of* MAGGIE *and one mistake is followed by others... musical and physical... threatening to put them all off their stride. It quickly unravels. They get to the end, however, and there is muted applause. They bow and leave the stage. The applause and the lights slowly fade.*

Lights up on DIANE *and* BRUNO *in the kitchen.* DIANE *doing her make-up in the mirror. He watches her. Pause.*

DIANE. Lipstick.

BRUNO *riffles through* DIANE*'s bag and takes out some lipstick. He hands it to her.*

Wrong one.

He takes it back and riffles through, finding another. He hands it to her. He continues to watch.

Thanks. Stop watching. You're making me nervous.

BRUNO. Why do you have more than one lipstick?

DIANE. Depends what mood I'm in.

BRUNO. So what mood is this?

DIANE (*reads off the side of the lipstick*). 'In the Pink'.

He laughs.

I'm going to drop in on Maggie later on.

BRUNO. What for?

DIANE. I haven't spoken to her for over a week. I just want to make sure she's alright.

BRUNO. Being on stage for the first time… Under those lights. If you're not used to that…

DIANE. None of us are used to it.

BRUNO. No but if you're not feeling a hundred per cent. Or fifty per cent even. Hardly surprising.

Pause.

I nailed it.

DIANE. You did.

BRUNO. That's the irony. It was far and away the best I've ever sung it. You know why?

DIANE. You had hundreds of people watching you?

BRUNO. No.

DIANE. Mascara please.

BRUNO. I was singing it to you.

DIANE. Ah.

She passes the lipstick back. He has another riffle through the bag.

BRUNO. I didn't even have to think about it. I 'became' the song. I've read about that but it's never happened…

He stops and takes something else out of the bag.

What's this?

He holds up a pregnancy test. Pause.

You're / not…

DIANE. No. It's old.

BRUNO *inspects it.*

BRUNO. Not that old.

DIANE. I needed to be sure.

BRUNO. Right. That would have been… awkward. To say the least. Have you been taking precautions?

DIANE. Have you?

BRUNO. No. You said that you were. Have you not?

DIANE (*beat*). Yes.

BRUNO. You have.

DIANE. Yes.

BRUNO. Sorry. Sorry. I panicked. Although as it happens...
I think we'd make a rather wonderful child.

DIANE. Do you? I think we would too. (*Beat*.) But... awkward.

BRUNO. Well... yes.

DIANE. A wonderful but awkward baby.

Pause.

Would it be so awful?

BRUNO. What?

DIANE. If I got pregnant.

BRUNO. I didn't say awful.

DIANE. For someone who claims to be in love with me?

BRUNO. I didn't say awful. And I don't claim to be in love with
you. I AM in love with you. But that doesn't mean I think we
should have a baby.

DIANE. You said once you wanted children.

BRUNO. Yes.

DIANE. And I would tell him.

BRUNO. Steven? What would you tell him?

DIANE. It depends. I could... I could pretend the baby was...
his. If you didn't / want...

BRUNO. Wait a minute, wait a minute. You're not pregnant.

DIANE. No.

BRUNO. You're quite sure.

DIANE. I have never been surer of anything in my life.

BRUNO. Right. So why are / we even...

DIANE. I'm just saying that if... I was. With you. By you.
I could.

BRUNO. You could what? Pretend the baby was his?

DIANE. It's not necessarily a problem. There is actually
a chance that the baby would be entirely white...

BRUNO. Do you know how small that chance is? And even if it
wasn't entirely black, the likelihood is it would be black-ish...

DIANE. I know, I know. Even so... if I thought it was yours
I wouldn't HAVE to tell him.

BRUNO. Wouldn't have to tell him what?

Pause.

WOULDN'T HAVE TO TELL HIM WHAT?

DIANE. Don't shout at me. Please... don't shout at me.

BRUNO. Wouldn't have to tell him what?

Pause.

DIANE. Steven and I are trying to have a baby. Using a donor.

BRUNO. What? Since when?

DIANE. We haven't actually started yet.

BRUNO. So... right. You wouldn't have to tell him anything.
Assuming colour isn't an issue. For you or for Steven.

DIANE. I don't want it to be.

BRUNO. You could get pregnant by me and never know it.
Never WANT to know it. Given the large number of sperm
that are going to be sloshing around your uterus.

DIANE. Excuse me!

Pause. She lets it go.

I'd like it to be yours. I could tell him that the baby was yours.
That you had agreed to natural insemination / and that...

BRUNO. Oh so never mind love, we haven't even been having sex, we've been having natural insemination.

DIANE. And that you were happy to be a sperm donor.

BRUNO. But I'm not.

DIANE. No if you were.

BRUNO. But I'm NOT. When did I ever, ever suggest to you that I might be? And for that matter when did YOU ever, ever suggest that you wanted me to be?

Pause.

Do you even like me?

DIANE. Yes! Yes! Of course I love you. That's what I'm saying. We could work something out, couldn't we. You could be a… I don't know… a co-parent.

BRUNO. I don't want to be a co-parent. Whatever that is.

DIANE. But you were the one who talked about other arrangements / and…

BRUNO. I want to be a father.

DIANE. Exactly! You said you wanted / kids. You said…

BRUNO. I do. I do. In about ten years.

DIANE. Ten years… but you'd be…

BRUNO. Forty. Yes. And?

DIANE. You didn't say that.

BRUNO. What about Steven? Do you think HE'LL be happy for me to be a sperm donor. A rather 'hands-on' sperm donor? Or did you think he'd just come round to it in time. This is insane. This is insane behaviour. I feel like I've been completely conned.

DIANE. Bruno…

BRUNO. I HAVE been completely conned. I'm not a lover. I'm not even loved. I'm just back-up for the sperm bank.

DIANE. No.

BRUNO. Belt and braces. How could you do that? After everything we have said and done. I don't know who the hell you are any more…

He walks out of the kitchen and out of the hall. Lights slowly fade on DIANE, motionless in the kitchen.

Lights up on the hall again. STEVEN, BEN and CONNIE have just arrived.

CONNIE. Here we are again.

BEN. Older and stupider.

CONNIE. If that's possible. I warned you. All of you.

BEN. Oh bugger!

STEVEN. What?

BEN. Your stamp. I could nip back and get it now if…

STEVEN. Ben… I'm sorry, I should have told you.

BEN. I thought that was a done deal.

STEVEN. We're having to spend our money elsewhere I'm afraid. I'm sorry.

BEN. Right. Of course. No worries. (*Laughs.*) It's only money. Have you guys started yet?

STEVEN. A week tomorrow.

CONNIE. Fingers crossed.

Pause.

Is she coming?

STEVEN. Maggie? No. At least we haven't told her.

BEN. Why not?

CONNIE. What happened to her mum? She never turned up, did she?

STEVEN. Apparently she got caught in traffic. Like us. Only she somehow missed the whole event.

CONNIE. Probably a good thing. I still can't believe they didn't even talk to us! We could have explained. That's how bad they thought we were. And we're not.

STEVEN. We weren't great. If truth be told. It made us look utterly incompetent.

BEN. It didn't.

CONNIE. We were good enough. Which is more than can be said for that contortionist. Who wants to see some nineteen-year-old wrap her ankles behind her neck?

BEN. Well…

CONNIE. Don't! Just don't.

BEN. What next then? *X Factor*? *The Voice*?

CONNIE. I'm not in the mood for singing if I'm honest.

DIANE *enters*.

BEN. That's exactly when you should sing.

CONNIE. No Bruno?

STEVEN. I'm afraid he's not coming.

BEN. Why not?

STEVEN. He's leaving the group.

CONNIE. What?

DIANE. Since when?

CONNIE. Why?

STEVEN. I'm not… I don't know exactly. He left a rather… garbled message yesterday. (*To* DIANE.) Did I not say?

DIANE. No.

CONNIE. That's a shame.

BEN. You'd think he'd come and tell us himself. After all this time.

DIANE. I imagine the whole Talentfest thing must have got to him.

STEVEN. Really? I'm afraid we've got some other bad news. (*Pause.*) About Maggie.

CONNIE. Oh no. Don't tell me things have…

STEVEN. No… no… quite the opposite actually. (*Beat.*) We don't think she has breast cancer.

BEN. That's good news, isn't it.

STEVEN. No. Well… yes. Except that we don't think she has ever had breast cancer.

CONNIE. What?

STEVEN. I've had my doubts for some time but then last week Diane ran into Maggie's neighbour.

DIANE. I asked if he'd seen her, if she was okay. I mentioned her mother and he said 'What mother?' That he hadn't seen anyone remotely resembling a mother. At any time.

STEVEN. I mean, just because no one has seen the mother doesn't mean there ISN'T one but… we think she's been lying.

DIANE. We KNOW.

BEN. Wait / a minute.

CONNIE. About her mother or about being ill?

DIANE. Both.

CONNIE. Why would anyone lie about that?

BEN. Are you seriously telling me she's got nothing wrong with her. And never has.

DIANE. Yes.

BEN. That is mental.

STEVEN. Yes.

DIANE. Literally.

BEN. How do you know?

STEVEN. Right. Firstly, Jan Watson left the NHS two years ago. She's listed online as having a private clinic in Kirkby. Not something Maggie could ever afford. Secondly…

BEN. She could be going to a private clinic, we don't know what funds she has or hasn't got...

STEVEN. Diane had to lend her money for God's sake! For childcare.

DIANE. Two thousand pounds!

STEVEN. TWO thousand?

DIANE. She needed it! That's what she said anyway.

CONNIE. That is disgusting.

BEN. She WOULD need it if she was having to pay for her treatment...

CONNIE. We take her in to the group, we offer all the help we can...

MAGGIE enters. She is wearing a headscarf small enough to show that she has lost all her hair.

MAGGIE. Yoo-hoo. Hello, everyone.

All staring at her.

I know, it looks a bit odd doesn't it. I keep wondering who the person in the mirror is. (*Beat.*) Oh dear. That bad. I didn't know whether you'd be here, I didn't get a message... and then I got all het up and thought that maybe, after what happened, you know... and then I bumped into Bruno. I completely understand if you'd rather I didn't come along any more but either way I just wanted to say face to face how sorry I am for what happened in Leeds.

BEN. No worries.

MAGGIE. I don't know what came over me.

STEVEN. Maggie...

MAGGIE. I think with all the treatment it was just all too much and then with one thing and another... I'm sorry. After all that work. I'm so so sorry.

No one moves.

BEN. Don't worry. Really. There are more important things to worry about.

DIANE. Yes.

MAGGIE. Don't I know it. I brought some Welsh cakes. If anyone's interested. Homemade of course. Oh and I almost forgot. Introductions are in order. Hello I'm Maggie and this is Thelma and this is Louise. (*Indicating her breasts*.)

Silence.

Like you said.

Silence.

So… no more Bruno.

STEVEN. No.

CONNIE. Nice scarf.

MAGGIE. It started coming out in clumps. Not a pretty sight, first thing in the morning. Hair all over the pillow. They did warn me.

DIANE (*beat*). It looks like you've shaved it.

MAGGIE. I have yes. Why?

DIANE. Just wondered.

MAGGIE. Jan told me that once it starts falling out it's a good idea to shave it. It makes you feel you're in control and not the poison. Is something wrong? (*Beat*.) You're all very angry with me, aren't you. I don't blame you.

STEVEN. We're all a bit… despondent to say / the least…

MAGGIE. I can't tell you how much I wish it hadn't happened…

CONNIE. We all wish that.

MAGGIE. If you'd rather I just went away…

Pause.

Only I'm getting weird feelings from all of you and I don't like it!

DIANE. Maggie… there's a couple of questions we'd like to ask.

MAGGIE. Questions. What kind of questions?

Silence. No one quite able to take the plunge.

CONNIE. Well here's one for a start. What does Jan Watson
look like?

MAGGIE. Jan? My consultant?

CONNIE. Yes.

MAGGIE. Why?

DIANE. Connie…

CONNIE. No, no let's not pussyfoot around. If you don't mind
just answer the question and then I'll tell you why.

MAGGIE. Well she's about… actually I think I do mind. I do
mind.

DIANE. Maggie, it would save us all an awful lot of pain and
a lot more / besides if you…

MAGGIE. Why would you ask me something like that? What
my consultant looks like. Who is nothing to do with you.
Nothing!

CONNIE. You don't know, do you.

MAGGIE. Of course I know.

CONNIE. So why don't you say?

Pause.

DIANE. Because of you I have spent a lot of the last two
months, revisiting a time of my life I would have much
preferred not to revisit. Because I… we wanted to help you.
And all of us have given… in different ways. And now…

Pause.

You don't have cancer, do you.

MAGGIE. What?

DIANE. You never have. You have been lying to us.

MAGGIE. How dare you?

CONNIE. Just tell us what Jan Watson looks like!

MAGGIE. I thought you were my friends.

BEN. We are.

MAGGIE. No you're not. Friends don't all gang up on each other. Calling each other liars.

BEN. Look, Maggie, Connie's asked you three times now, each time you don't answer, it doesn't look good...

MAGGIE. Jan Watson is my consultant. I've been seeing her for the last three months.

STEVEN. At the hospital?

MAGGIE. What does it matter WHERE I see her. And of course I know what she looks like!

CONNIE. Then tell us.

MAGGIE. You think it's not bad enough having cancer, having bits of your breast lopped off, or wondering how you're going to cope with a small child, or whether you're going to live or die? Why are you doing this to me?

DIANE. I phoned the hospital, Maggie. First off, Jan Watson doesn't work there any more. In fact she's stopped working for the NHS altogether. She only sees private patients.

MAGGIE. So? I've been seeing her privately...

STEVEN. You've been paying for private treatment?

MAGGIE. Yes! I mean obviously I've got insurance. If you really want to know. Not that it's any / of your business.

DIANE. Jan Watson is...

CONNIE. Thank God for the NHS you said, I remember it...

MAGGIE. No I didn't.

CONNIE. 'Thank God for the NHS.'

BEN. Steven said it to be fair.

CONNIE. And she agreed!

MAGGIE. Yes and I meant it. That doesn't mean I can't be a private patient, does it? You've no idea what it's like, have you. No idea who I am or... you're like a pack of wolves.

And if you think I'm going to stand here while you all point the finger at me. I came here for help. For support. And instead you do this to me. It's disgusting. Disgusting! (*To* DIANE.) And you of all people.

DIANE. Maggie…

MAGGIE. Not another word. I don't want to hear. I do NOT WANT TO HEAR!

She exits. Silence.

STEVEN. Jesus.

BEN. That was horrible.

STEVEN (*to* DIANE). Are you alright?

DIANE (*distraught*). I'm not sure I can do this.

CONNIE. She wouldn't answer because she couldn't. She knows that Diane knows what Jan Watson looks like. Otherwise she would have said something.

BEN. Unless she was genuinely offended.

BRUNO enters.

BRUNO. What's going on? Maggie's outside bawling her eyes out. She says you've all / accused her of…

CONNIE. We know what Maggie says, she's a nasty little liar.

STEVEN. We weren't expecting to see you.

BRUNO. If you make an accusation like that you need to be absolutely certain. Because if you are wrong, you are going to hell.

CONNIE. She doesn't know what her own doctor looks like!

Suddenly MAGGIE *re-enters.*

MAGGIE. You know I didn't ask to join your stupid little group. With your stupid little jokes… I didn't even ask if I could sing for Talentfest. I did it as a favour. You really think I haven't got better things to do with my time? Than to sit and listen to your sad little… I've got a son. (*To* DIANE.)

You wouldn't know about that. What that means. What you have to do for them. And when there's no one to help. You think you're all so special and clever, don't you. But you're not! You're not even clever enough to make up your own songs even! You just copy other people! You're like everyone else! Only not as good. And just so you know... Jan Watson is forty-eight years old, wears glasses and has dark brown curly hair. Happy?

Silence.

BEN. Is that right?

DIANE *nods.*

Oh shit!

Pause.

Oh shit. Maggie, I am SO / sorry –

STEVEN (*to* MAGGIE). What were you doing out there?

MAGGIE. What?

STEVEN (*to* BRUNO). What was she doing out there?

BRUNO. When?

STEVEN. Just now.

MAGGIE. Stop it!

BRUNO. She was on her phone.

STEVEN. Making a call?

BRUNO. No just...

STEVEN. Googling.

MAGGIE. Why are you doing this to me?

STEVEN. You googled her.

MAGGIE. I've done nothing wrong.

DIANE. Jan Watson has been on sabbatical for the last year.

MAGGIE. Not true.

DIANE. She is currently travelling in Vietnam.

MAGGIE. Not true!

DIANE. Maggie, you are lying!

Silence.

MAGGIE (*desperate*). She Skypes.

DIANE. She 'Skypes'. From Vietnam. Every week. Is that right?

MAGGIE *frozen.*

(*On the verge of meltdown.*) Well you may not be prepared to confess but I am. Because although I haven't abused your trust. Although I haven't taken money off you under false pretences. And I haven't fabricated stories about myself just so that I could revel in your sympathy. I have nonetheless lied to you. I lied about my sister Carol. About my own twin sister. Full recovery? Jesus Christ, if only. I lied just so as you wouldn't be frightened! You fucking little bitch!

She breaks down. STEVEN *immediately goes to her aid and sits her down.*

STEVEN (*to* MAGGIE). I think you'd better leave.

MAGGIE *still frozen.*

Now!

MAGGIE. I hate you. I hate all of you.

She exits.

CONNIE. Dear God. Is that it? Are we just going to let her walk out?

BRUNO. What else can we do?

DIANE. We should report her to the authorities.

BEN. What, for lying?

STEVEN. If we support her when she's got cancer we can hardly tear her to pieces when she's got... factitious disorder or whatever.

CONNIE. 'Factitious disorder.' That's not an illness. That's just a PC way of saying she's a fucking liar. She knows what she's doing. You don't choose to have cancer. But you choose to tell a bloody lie.

BRUNO. She's sick.

BEN. Not necessarily…

STEVEN. Mad, bad or sad. Take your pick. I think she is mentally ill.

CONNIE. Are you telling me she doesn't know what she's doing is wrong?

BRUNO. No idea. What do you think, Diane?

DIANE *heads for the door.*

STEVEN. Where are you going?

DIANE. I need some air.

She exits.

STEVEN. Even if Maggie does know, she's clearly not in control of it.

CONNIE. Course she knows. Why? Because she wanted to join the group. Simple as.

STEVEN. It's not as / simple as that.

CONNIE. She's not 'got' anything. She wanted to do Talentfest and knew she didn't stand a dog's chance. So instead she ruins it for all of us. She tricked us. Typical. Typical fucking Taff.

BEN. Connie, come on

CONNIE. 'They pray on their knees and their neighbours.' Too bloody right. And don't give me that touchy-feely rubbish about… You know what… I hope she bloody GETS cancer!

BEN. Connie!

BRUNO. What!

STEVEN. You don't mean that.

CONNIE (*tearful*). I do. She wrecked our chances at that audition. And we took her in! Out of the goodness of our hearts! We took her in. And we would have won that competition.

BRUNO. You don't know that.

CONNIE. WE WOULD HAVE WON IT! And we'd have gone on and who knows. Our lives could have changed. Just like that.

She starts to move to the door.

No! Sorry but it's not right...

BEN. Where are you going?

CONNIE. No way am I just going to let her walk / out of here...

BEN. Connie...

CONNIE. ...like nothing's happened, no bloody way...

She exits.

BEN. Connie!

He follows her out as speed. BRUNO *is left alone with* STEVEN. *An awkward silence.*

BRUNO. Bloody hell.

STEVEN. Bloody hell indeed.

Pause.

BRUNO. Did you tell everyone?

STEVEN. Tell everyone what?

BRUNO. That I was moving on.

STEVEN. Oh yes. I did.

BRUNO. Thanks. I just thought that it's been a year now and maybe / the time had...

STEVEN. Don't demean yourself, Bruno.

BRUNO. What?

STEVEN. You know, when Diane's sister died, nine-and-a-half years ago, Diane had a breakdown. She just tipped into a place of utter despair. Grief. Survivor's guilt. Everything. I didn't realise at first. How bad it was. I went away on some choir outing and when I got back she had drawn all the curtains, hadn't flushed the loo for a week. It was a kind of madness where I lost her altogether. And I vowed there and then, for her sake AND mine, that however bad things were, whatever... difficulties we got in to, I would keep her on an even keel. Nothing, NOTHING would ever take us back to that place. In fact that's why I started the group. I thought it might help heal her in some way. And it did.

BRUNO (*beat*). Right.

Pause.

STEVEN. Do you love her? (*Beat.*) I doubt it. Infatuation maybe. But not love. It's the difference between a Steinway and a Casio keyboard. In case you were wondering. One has depth and quality and history. The other just has flashing lights and novelty value. And breaks very easily. I know she doesn't love you. Though she probably thinks she does given her situation...

BRUNO. Steven...

STEVEN. Perhaps she thought that by agreeing to accept the sperm of a total stranger I somehow wouldn't mind if she shifted the goalposts a little.

BRUNO. Steven, I really...

STEVEN, THIS HAS TO BE SAID! So shut up! (*Beat.*) It's obviously been as hard for her to imagine the depth of my unhappiness at discovering her infidelity as it has been for me to imagine her desperation to have a child. Either way it's not the thought of you having sex with my wife, behind my back AND under my nose, that upsets me most. It's the tiny lies that go with it. The calculated ones. That spread and keep on spreading... like cells starting to mutate, until they form clusters and do real, irreparable damage. I don't know if I've caught it in time. I don't suppose with all those flashing lights that you thought about any of that.

BRUNO. I'm sorry.

STEVEN. We haven't had this conversation.

DIANE *enters with* BEN *and* CONNIE.

BEN. Couldn't see her for dust.

CONNIE. No surprises there.

STEVEN. Bruno's just leaving.

BRUNO. For good.

BEN. So we gather.

CONNIE. Her fault as well.

BRUNO. No.

CONNIE. She's knocked the stuffing out of everything. God help her if I ever meet her in the street.

BEN. She's a nutter. Let go.

BRUNO. Mum's getting more demanding. And things are getting busy at school. Exams and tests. I'm getting all kinds of stuff thrown at me. I think it's for the best.

CONNIE. Ah. (*Giving him a hug.*) Won't be the same without you. Will it, Steven?

STEVEN. It certainly won't.

BEN. Does that mean I get to sing his solos?

CONNIE. We'll see you around and about anyway.

BRUNO. Of course.

BEN. Alright, mate, take care…

BRUNO. Goodbye, Diane.

DIANE. Bye.

CONNIE. You can always change your mind.

BRUNO *leaves.*

BEN. Are we going to try and replace him?

STEVEN. I don't know. (*To* DIANE.) What do you think? Is he replaceable? Can we do without another Bruno?

DIANE. See how it goes.

STEVEN. Let's make a move. I don't think any of us are in a fit state to do any singing today.

They gather their things.

Will you two lock up?

BEN. Haven't got the key.

CONNIE *rummages in her bag, looking for the key. Before she can find it,* STEVEN *produces a key from his own pocket.*

STEVEN. I had an extra one made. Hang on to it.

CONNIE. Good luck for next week.

STEVEN. Thanks. (*To* DIANE.) All set?

DIANE *eyes fixed on the key.*

Diane?

She nods. They exit. CONNIE *despondent.*

BEN. It's not the end of the world, you know.

CONNIE. No, worse luck. It's the same old, bloody world. I wanted some excitement, that's all. Is that such a crime? I wanted to… what's that film…

BEN. Oh God…

CONNIE. With the big fella… well he was by the end anyway.

BEN. Orson Welles?

CONNIE. No. Bigger.

BEN. Shrek?

CONNIE. Brando. Marlon Brando…

BEN. Oh that Brando…

CONNIE. When he's all bashed up…

BEN. You wanted to be a contender.

CONNIE. Yeah, that's it. I wanted to BE someone. Don't you?

BEN. I AM someone, thanks very much.

CONNIE. Oh yes, you can't even sell a postage stamp, for God's sake. We're not moving house either, are we.

BEN. No.

CONNIE. Knew it.

Pause.

BEN. You know what… I didn't get injured on purpose all those years ago. It wasn't my choice. It's just what happened. Sometimes life does that. And you either carry it with you like a stone in your shoe for the rest of your life or you move on. But if you want to know the truth I was never going to make it into the top one hundred. Three hundred maybe.

CONNIE. You don't know that. You could have been Andy Murray.

BEN. Not even Jamie Murray. Outclassed in every possible way. Buster Mottram at a pinch.

CONNIE. Who?

BEN. Exactly. And, you know, if I'm not good enough for you, then maybe you should stop whinging and move on.

CONNIE. I didn't say that.

BEN. You say it every day.

They stare at each other.

But I was right when I saw your bum on that poster. The top half was just as good as the bottom half. Still is.

CONNIE. I wish you'd tell me that more often. Instead of…

BEN. I think it. I do think it.

CONNIE. Well how about thinking it out loud.

Silence.

Come on… you'll miss the football.

BEN. What football?

CONNIE. God knows. Isn't there always football?

BEN. No.

CONNIE. Christ. Might just have to talk to each other.

She leaves. He follows.

MAGGIE *appears centre stage.*

MAGGIE. In the end I thought it best to move again. Shame really as Jack had got settled into his new school. He's only eleven. Bless him. Growing up fast, mind. And that's another thing. Last week… (*Getting upset.*) it was a school day it was and usually me and him we walk together to the school gates, he carries his bag and I carry his packed lunch, have a little chat on the way and then when we get to the gates, I give him his lunch and a little hug, say goodbye and off he goes… only last… Thursday I think it was… when we left the house, HE wanted to carry his packed lunch so I thought, fine, no skin off my nose, and I gave it to him. Only… only then he asked me not to come with him… said he wanted to go to school on his own. Didn't want the hug either. So now I just watch him through the window. Till he turns the corner.

Pause.

You know it's a funny thing… when it's quiet… like sometimes in the middle of the night… I do wonder. I wonder if what happened was somehow my fault. But then in the morning I wake up and remember all the things they said… and my blood begins to boil. I'm sure that's why all this nonsense started. With the heart. I say the heart but no one here seems to know for certain. I asked to see Derek again… Dr Battle. I think men know better somehow, don't you? When it's things that you can't see. Things inside. I've got them all quite flummoxed. All those white coats rushing round. Scratching their heads. What did they call me at the surgery? An enigma. That's it. (*Laughs.*) I quite like that. An enigma. Yes I suppose I am.

The lights fade on her.

The End.

www.nickhernbooks.co.uk

facebook.com/nickhernbooks

twitter.com/nickhernbooks